Principles of the Spin Model Checker

Mordechai Ben-Ari

Principles of the Spin Model Checker

 Springer

Mordechai Ben-Ari, BSc, MSc, PhD
Weizmann Institute of Science
Rehovot 76100
Israel

ISBN: 978-1-84628-769-5   e-ISBN: 978-1-84628-770-1

British Library Cataloguing in Publication Data
A catalogue record for this book is available from the British Library

Library of Congress Control Number: 2007941384

Printed on acid-free paper

9 8 7 6 5 4 3 2 1

Springer Science+Business Media
springer.com

Foreword

Anyone who has tried to write a nontrivial piece of software knows from bitter experience that the code is not likely to work quite right after the first successful compilation; nor the second or third. Sometimes, it takes a while to discover how a seemingly correct program can fail in subtle ways. The same is of course true for commercially developed software. Small flaws can hide for years and strike at the most inconvenient moment. So we learn to backup our data and cope with the apparently inevitable. There are, however, cases where we do not have the luxury of accepting products that may be subtly flawed. In some applications, software defects can lead to a loss of life or cause significant economical damage. Given that so much of our world is now controlled by software, finding ways to make this software more reliable is perhaps the most important technical challenge of our age. So, how can we accomplish this?

Most critical software applications execute in a multithreaded environment, with numerous external dependencies: they are concurrent. It is especially the concurrency aspects – the mutual dependencies – that are difficult to get right. Fortunately, today powerful tools are available to verify the logical correctness of concurrent (distributed, parallel, or multithreaded) programs. SPIN is perhaps the leading example of such a tool. Its development dates back to roughly 1980, with a first free version publicly released in 1991. It is often considered to be one of the most powerful model checkers available.

SPIN is increasingly used in the classroom to teach concurrency and model checking techniques, but, most important, it is applied in industrial practice to solve real problems in the construction of large-scale distributed software systems. The tool has been used for the verification of everything from operating systems software and communications protocols to railway signaling systems. Some of the larger applications are especially inspiring. In the late 90s, for instance, SPIN was used to verify the control algorithms for a large new flood control system near Rotterdam in The Netherlands. It was used between 1999 and 2001 at Bell Laboratories to verify the call processing software for a new telephone switch. And, finally, SPIN is used increasingly for a thorough verification of key control algorithms for interplanetary space missions at NASA.

So far, most publications on the SPIN system have focused on its theoretical background, with less attention being paid to routine usage and application. This book offers for the first time a comprehensive introduction to SPIN from a user's perspective. It makes the capabilities of the tool accessible to a much broader audience. All key concepts are explained step-by-step, without fuss, in a clear and instructive way that can get the reader up to speed very quickly. As such, this book has no competition. This is the best introduction to the SPIN tool.

Gerard J. Holzmann
Pasadena, California
May 2007

Preface

Surrounded as we are by software for personal computers, electronic gadgets and entertainment websites, it is easy to lose sight of the massive amount of software embedded in critical systems. I was surprised when I found out that the computerized systems in modern cars have half a million lines of code, and that electronics account for 25% of their cost and this percentage is forecast to increase.[1] Perhaps it is easiest to characterize a critical system as one that must be delivered without one of those infamous "end user license agreements" that disavows liability and requires you to renounce any claim to a guarantee.

Formal methods are powerful tools in the arsenal of software engineers who develop software that *must* work correctly. While the principles of formal methods were developed decades ago by pioneers of computer science like C.A.R. Hoare and the late E.W. Dijkstra, only recently have theoretical advances and progress in the development of software tools enabled their widespread use.

Model checking

One of the most powerful formal methods is *model checking*. In principle model checking is trivial: simply generate all possible states of a program and check that the correctness specifications hold in each state. Furthermore, generating states and checking specifications can be done mechanically by a software tool. In practice, sophisticated algorithms based upon automata theory and logic are needed to perform model checking on nontrivial programs which have billions or trillions of states.

---

[1] Klaus Grimm. Software technology in an automotive company – Major challenges, *Proceedings of the 25th International Conference on Software Engineering*, 2003, 498–503.

Even the best model checkers are not "plug and play": If a program has even one 32-bit integer variable, at each location during the execution of the program that variable can give rise to as many as 2^{32} different states. As the name implies, model checkers do not check *programs*, but rather *models*, which are high level descriptions of a system. The challenge for a software engineer is to develop a model that faithfully represents the system, while at the same time remaining sufficiently concise to enable its correctness to be checked with the available resources. The complementary challenge for designers of model checkers is to include sufficiently expressive constructs to facilitate the construction of faithful models, while leaving out constructs that cannot be efficiently implemented.

SPIN

SPIN is a model checker developed by Gerard J. Holzmann for verifying communications protocols. It has since become widely used in industries that build critical systems. In 2001, Holzmann received the ACM Software Systems Award for the development of SPIN. My interest in SPIN arose from my long-time engagement in teaching concurrent programming. Pieter Hartel convinced me to look into SPIN, and I found that SPIN is a very rare artifact: Although it is an industrial-strength tool, it can be easily used by students. The software is simple to install and to run, and models are written in PROMELA, which looks like a familiar programming language.

This led to my writing a new edition of the textbook *Principles of Concurrent and Distributed Programming* (Ben-Ari, 2006), which included material on SPIN. In addition, I built pedagogical software tools that leverage the capabilities of SPIN. I have come to believe that SPIN can be used to introduce students to important concepts in computer science, such as logic, automata, concurrency, nondeterminism, and program verification.

The only impediment I found to the wider use of SPIN in computer science education was the lack of an introductory book. *The Spin Model Checker: Primer and Reference Manual* (Holzmann, 2004) contains, in addition to elementary explanations, a wealth of material on the theory and implementation of SPIN, and on the design and verification of models for communications systems. As such, beginners might find it difficult to use as an introductory text.

Principles of the Spin Model Checker is intended as an introduction to SPIN for undergraduate students and for programmers without a strong background in formal methods. It presents the concepts of model checking, the constructs of PROMELA, and the capabilities of SPIN comprehensively, but in steps of gradually increasing difficulty. The book is self-contained, but will probably be accessible only to readers with two or three years of programming experience. An elementary knowledge of logic – the propositional calculus – is also required; see my textbook *Mathematical Logic for Computer Science* (Ben-Ari, 2004) if you need help.

The book describes SPIN-based software tools that I have developed: the JSPIN development environment, SPINSPIDER for visualizing state diagrams, and VN for experiencing nondeterminism.

Of course, once you actually start to work with SPIN, you will want to consult *The Spin Model Checker* and the *man* pages.[2]

Overview of the book

Principles of the Spin Model Checker is organized into three parts. Chapters 1 through 5 introduce the main concepts that are needed to write models in PROMELA and to verify them with SPIN. Chapters 6 and 7 present structures in PROMELA that are essential for constructing models, while Chapters 8–11 include more advanced and optional material.

Models in SPIN are written in the PROMELA language; its syntax is based upon that of C, but it is sufficiently different that it seems worthwhile to give a gentle introduction to PROMELA and SPIN using *sequential* programs (Chapter 1). This is followed in Chapter 2 by an introduction to verification, again within the context of sequential programs. SPIN is primarily used for modeling and verifying concurrent systems, and this is presented in Chapter 3 on modeling multiprocess systems, in Chapter 4 on the synchronization of processes, and in Chapter 5 on linear temporal logic that is used to express correctness specifications in SPIN.

Chapter 6 is concerned with constructs for structuring data and programs, and Chapter 7 explains channels, which are used for modeling distributed systems, as well as for implementing data structures.

Chapter 8 diverges from the usual view of model checkers as tools for verifying concurrent and distributed systems. It shows how SPIN can be used to teach the important concept of nondeterminism that appears in many contexts in computer science, such as algorithms and automata. Chapter 9 presents advanced PROMELA constructs and Chapter 10 surveys advanced capabilities of SPIN for expressing correctness specifications and for optimizing verifications.

The book concludes with five cases studies in Chapter 11 designed to bring together the individual PROMELA programming structures that were

---

[2] *man* pages form the definitive documentation. They can be found in Chapters 16–19 of the *The Spin Model Checker* (Holzmann, 2004) and online at the SPIN website; they can also be downloaded with the SPIN distribution.

presented in isolation: (a) the implementation of a complex data structure; (b) further examples of nondeterministic algorithms; (c) a real-time scheduling algorithm; (d) a model that uses discrete time; (e) an advanced algorithm for a distributed system.

Appendix A gives an overview of the software tools I have developed. For details see the documentation included within the archive for each tool. Appendix B contains the addresses of relevant websites. A short list of references will direct you to more advanced books.

Instructions for running SPIN are given in two forms: (a) using the JSPIN environment, and (b) commands and arguments for running SPIN directly from the command line.

The source code of all the PROMELA programs in the book is available on the companion website at www.springer.com/978-1-84628-769-5.

Conventions

Starred (*) sections can be skipped on your first reading and returned to later on. Framed text is used to emphasize important warnings. Passages marked **Advanced** can be safely passed over by most readers. Acronyms are used for several books referred to frequently: *SMC* for Holzmann (2004), *MLCS* for Ben-Ari (2004), and *PCDP* for Ben-Ari (2006).

Acknowledgements

I am deeply indebted to Gerard J. Holzmann for his support and help during the writing of *PCDP* and of this book, and during the development of my software tools. I am grateful to Angelika Mader for carefully reading the manuscript; her eagle eye for obscure explanations significantly improved the presentation. Thanks also to Pieter Hartel for introducing me to SPIN, Michal Armoni for collaborating on the VN software, and Dragan Bošnački for help with modeling discrete time. Finally, it has been a pleasure to work with Beverley Ford and the entire staff at Springer.

Mordechai Ben-Ari
Rehovot
June 2007

Contents

Sequential Programming in PROMELA

SPIN is a *model checker* – a software tool for verifying models of physical systems, in particular, computerized systems. First, a model is written that describes the behavior of the system; then, correctness properties that express requirements on the system's behavior are specified; finally, the model checker is run to check if the correctness properties hold for the model, and, if not, to provide a counterexample: a computation that does not satisfy a correctness property. Model checking is challenging and fascinating because one must write a model that describes the system in sufficient detail to represent it faithfully, and yet the model must be sufficiently simple so that the model checker can perform the verification with the available resources (time and memory).

Our goal is to learn how to perform model checking in SPIN. We start with the first stage: learning the PROMELA language that is used for writing models in SPIN. PROMELA is, in effect, a simple programming language, so we will show how to use PROMELA to write sequential programs, and then gradually introduce the constructs used for performing verification and for writing models of real systems.

1.1 A first program in PROMELA

Assignment statements and expressions in PROMELA are written using the syntax of C-like languages. Listing 1.1 is a trivial program that reverses the digits of a three-digit number. Programs in PROMELA are composed of a set of *processes*; here we start with a single process declared by the words **active proctype**. Processes may have parameters, though we shall not use them until much later; even if there are no parameters, the parentheses ()

must appear. The statements of the process are written between the braces { and }. Comments are enclosed between /* and */.

Listing 1.1. Reversing digits

```
1   active proctype P() {
2     int value = 123; /* Try with a byte variable here ... */
3     int reversed;      /* ... and here! */
4     reversed =
5       (value % 10) * 100 +
6       ((value / 10) % 10) * 10 +
7       (value / 100);
8     printf("value = %d, reversed = %d\n", value, reversed)
9   }
```

In the program we declared two variables, value and reversed, of type **int**, the first of which is given an explicit initial value. The value assigned to the variable reversed is computed from the value of the variable value using the division and modulo operators; then, the values of both variables are printed. The **printf** statement is taken from the C language: a quoted string followed by a list of variables; the list of variables should match the *format specifiers* embedded within the string. The specifier for printing integer values is %d, and the string can be terminated by the newline character \n.

If you run a random simulation of this program as described in the next section, SPIN will print:

```
value = 123, reversed = 321
```

Advanced: Single-line comments

The single line comment from // until the end of the line is not normally available in SPIN unless you use a different preprocessor; this is explained in the *man* page for macros.

1.2 Random simulation

In simulation mode, SPIN compiles and executes a PROMELA program. Here we discuss random simulation mode; the meaning of "random" in this context will be apparent later.

By convention, we use the extension pml for PROMELA files.

To run a random simulation:

jSpin

Select Open (ctrl-O) to load a file into the editor window, or File / New to create a new file. Edit the program and save the file (File / Save (ctrl-S)). A message that the file has been saved appears in the message pane at the bottom of the frame. It is not necessary to explicitly save files as this is automatically done before executing SPIN.

Select Random (alt-R). SPIN will compile and execute the program, and the compile-time errors or the output from the execution will appear in the right pane.

You may wish to perform a syntax check before running the program: select Check (alt-K).

By default, JSPIN displays the state of the program after executing each instruction; for running the first simple programs in this book turn this output off by selecting Options / Common / Clear all / OK and then Options/Save to save the changes.

Command line

Run:

    spin filename

Output will be printed on standard output and can be redirected or piped.

You can set a limit on the number of steps that will be executed in a simulation run; this will be especially important when we discuss concurrent programs that need not terminate.

jSpin

Select Settings / Max steps (ctrl-M) and enter a value.

Command line

Run SPIN with the parameter -uN, where N is the maximum number of steps.

Advanced: Filtering output in jSpin

JSPIN can be used to filter the output so that only the results of certain **printf** statements are displayed. Change the configuration file
option MSC to true. Then only lines beginning with the string "MSC:"
will be displayed. This prefix is also used to display process interactions in the *Message Sequence Charts* of XSPIN; see Chapter 12 of *SMC*.

Advanced: Input in Promela

By convention, a PROMELA program does not have input, since it is
intended for simulating a *closed* system. That is, if there is a some
unit in the environment that could influence the system, it should be
modeled as a process. Nevertheless, there is an input channel STDIN
connected to standard input that can be useful for running simulations of a single model with different parameters; see the *man* pages.

1.3 Data types

The numeric data types of PROMELA are based upon those of the C compiler
used to compile SPIN itself; they are currently as shown in Table 1.1.[1] All
effort should be made to model data using types that need as few bits as
possible to avoid combinatorial explosion in the number of states during a
verification: **short** instead of **int** and **byte** instead of **short**.

Table 1.1. Numeric data types in PROMELA

Type	Values	Size (bits)
bit, bool	0, 1, **false**, **true**	1
byte	0..255	8
short	$-32768..32767$	16
int	$-2^{31}..2^{31} - 1$	32
unsigned	$0..2^n - 1$	≤ 32

The type **bool** and the values **true** and **false** are syntactic sugar for the
type **bit** and the values 1 and 0, respectively.[2] Values of type **bit** and **bool**
can be printed only as integer values with specifier %d.

---

[1] The other data types in PROMELA are: **chan** (Chapter 7), **pid** (Section 3.5), and
mtype (Section 1.4.2).

[2] *Syntactic sugar* is a term for alternate syntactic constructs that add no additional
capabilities to a programming language, but instead are intended to enable more

> ## Warning
>
> All variables are initialized by default to zero, but it is recom-
> mended that explicit initial values always be given in variable
> declarations.

PROMELA *does not* have some familiar data types:

- There is no separate character type in PROMELA. Literal character values can be assigned to variables of type **byte** and printed using the %c format specifier.
- There are no string variables in PROMELA. Messages are best modeled using just a few numeric codes and the full text is not needed. In any case, **printf** statements are only used as a convenience during simulation and are ignored when SPIN performs a verification.
- There are no floating-point data types in PROMELA. Floating-point numbers are generally not needed in models because the exact values are not important; it is better to model a numeric variable by a handful of discrete values such as minimum, low, high, maximum.[3]

Advanced: Initial values of variables

The recommendation to give explicit initial values is driven not only by good programming practice; it can also affect the size of models in SPIN. For example, if you need to model *positive* integer values and write

```
byte n;
n = 1;
```

there will be additional (and unnecessary) states in which the value of n is zero.

Advanced: Unsigned integer type

The type **unsigned** can be used for variables intended to hold unsigned values of a specified number of bits. It is meaningful when compression of the state vector is used. See *SMC* Chapter 3 and the *man* page for datatypes.

---

readable programs to be written. It is easier to read a program that contains **bool** done = **false** than **bit** done = 0, although there is no semantic difference whatsoever between them.

[3] If floating-point numbers are truly needed you can use them in embedded segments of C code. SPIN can verify a model with embedded C code on the assumption that this code is correct. See Chapter 17 of *SMC*.

1.3.1 Type conversions

There are no explicit type conversions in PROMELA. Arithmetic is *always* performed by first implicitly converting all values to **int**; upon assignment, the value is implicitly converted to the type of the variable. In our first program, if the variable value is declared to be of type **byte**, the program is still correct because the computation is performed on integers and then assigned to the variable reversed of type **int**. If, however, reversed is declared to be of type **byte**, the attempt to assign 321 to that variable will not succeed; the value will be truncated and an error message printed:

```
Error: value (321->65 (8)) truncated in assignment
value = 123, reversed = 65
```

You may be surprised that the error does not cause an exception or the termination of the program and that the truncated value is printed. SPIN leaves it up to you to decide if the truncated value is meaningful or not.

1.4 Operators and expressions

The set of operators in PROMELA, together with their precedence and associativity, is shown in Table 1.2; the operators are almost identical to those in C-like languages. Needless to say, it is not a good idea to try to memorize the table, but rather to use parentheses liberally to clarify precedence and associativity within expressions!

The following rule is central to the design of PROMELA:

Warning

Expressions in PROMELA must be side-effect free.

The reason for the rule is that expressions are used to determine if a statement is executable or not (Section 4.2), so it must be possible to evaluate an expression without side effects.

This requirement leads to several differences between PROMELA and the C language; in PROMELA

- Assignment statements are not expressions.
- The increment and decrement operators (++, --) may only be used as *postfix* operators in an assignment statement like:

    b++

Table 1.2. Operators in Promela

Precedence	Operator	Associativity	Name
14	( )	left	parentheses
14	[ ]	left	array indexing
14	.	left	field selection
13	!	right	logical negation
13	~	right	bitwise complementation
13	++, --	right	increment, decrement
12	*, /, %	left	multiplication, division, modulo
11	+, -	left	addition, subtraction
10	<<, >>	left	left and right bitwise shift
9	<, <=, >, >=	left	arithmetic relational operators
8	==, !=	left	equality, inequality
7	&	left	bitwise and
6	^	left	bitwise exclusive or
5	|	left	bitwise inclusive or
4	&&	left	logical and
3	||	left	logical or
2	(-> :)	right	conditional expression
1	=	right	assignment

and not in an expression like the right-hand side of an assignment statement:

```
a = b++
```

- There are no *prefix* increment and decrement operators. (Even if there were, there could be no difference between them and the postfix operators because they cannot be used in expressions.)

1.4.1 Local variables

The scope of a local variable is the entire process in which it is declared.

Warning

It is not necessary to declare variables at the beginning of a process; however, all variable declarations are implicitly moved to the beginning of the process.

This can have weird effects if you are used to the style in the JAVA language of declaring and initializing variables in the middle of a computation; for example:

```
byte a = 1;
   . . .
a = 5;
byte b = a+2;
printf("b= %d\n", b);
```

The output is 3. The variable b is implicitly declared *immediately after* the declaration of a; therefore, the expression a+2 uses the initial value 1.

1.4.2 Symbolic names*

If you just need to declare a symbol for a number, a preprocessor macro can be used at the beginning of the program:

```
#define N 10
```

Textual substitution is used when the symbol is encountered:

```
i = j % N;
```

The type **mtype** can be used to give mnemonic names to values (Listing 1.2).[4] The advantage of using **mtype** over a sequence of **#define**'s is that the symbolic values can be printed using the %e format specifier, and they will appear in traces of programs.

Internally, the values of the **mtype** are represented as *positive* byte values, so there can be at most 255 values of the type.

A limitation on **mtype** is that there is only one set of names defined for an entire program; if you add declarations, the new symbols are added to the existing set. Listing 1.3 shows how to add states for traffic signals in which two lights are on simultaneously (as is done in many countries).

Advanced: Printing values of mtype

The **printm** statement can be used to print a value of an **mtype**. See the *man* pages for **mtype** and **printf** for an explanation of when to use this instead of the format specifier %e.

---

[4] The term is short for *message type* because its original use was to give symbolic names instead of numbers to messages.

Listing 1.2. Symbolic names

```
1  mtype = { red, yellow, green };
2  mtype light = green;
3
4  active proctype P() {
5    do
6    :: if
7       :: light == red -> light = green
8       :: light == yellow -> light = red
9       :: light == green -> light = yellow
10      fi;
11      printf("The light is now %e\n", light)
12   od
13 }
```

Listing 1.3. Adding new symbolic names

```
1  mtype = { red, yellow, green };
2  mtype = { green_and_yellow, yellow_and_red };
3  mtype light = green;
4
5  active proctype P() {
6    do
7    :: if
8       :: light == red -> light = yellow_and_red
9       :: light == yellow_and_red -> light = green
10      :: light == green -> light = green_and_yellow
11      :: light == green_and_yellow -> light = red
12      fi;
13      printf("The light is now %e\n", light)
14   od
15 }
```

1.5 Control statements

While the syntax and semantics of expressions in PROMELA are taken from C-like languages, the control statements are taken from a formalism called *guarded commands* invented by E.W. Dijkstra. This formalism is particularly well suited for expressing nondeterminism and thus is a good match for modeling systems like communication systems that are by nature nondeterministic. We will treat nondeterminism at length in Chapter 8.

There are five control statements: sequence, selection, repetition, jump, and **unless**; the first four are presented here, while **unless** is described in Section 9.4.

The semicolon is the *separator* between statements that are executed in sequence. Semicolons are used as separators in the Pascal language, but most readers are probably more familiar with their use as terminators of statements in C-like languages. Fewer semicolons are needed when they are used as separators, so the code looks cleaner. Don't worry if you use an unnecessary semicolon, as SPIN will rarely complain.

Terminology: When a processor executes a program, a register called a *location counter* maintains the address of the next instruction that can be executed.[5] An address of an instruction is called a *control point*. For example, in PROMELA the sequence of statements

```
x = y + 2;
z = x * y;
printf("x = %d, z = %d\n", x, z)
```

has three control points, one before each statement, and the location counter of a process can be at any one of them.

1.6 Selection statements

The classic **if**-statement is based upon sequential checking of expressions until one evaluates to true, at which point the associated sequence of statements is executed. The sequential nature can be seen from the use of the keyword **else** in languages like JAVA or C:

---

[5] Other terms for *location counter* are *program counter (pc)* and *instruction pointer (ip)*.

```
if (expression-1) {
    statement-1-1; statement-1-2; statement-1-3;
}
else if (expression-2) {
    statement-2-1;
}
else {
    statement-3-1; statement-3-2;
}
```

In SPIN there is no semantic meaning to the order of the alternatives; the semantics of the statement merely says that if the expression of an alternative is true, the sequence of statements that follows it *can be* executed. The program in Listing 1.4 contains an **if**-statement that checks the discriminant of a quadratic equation; the three expressions are mutually exclusive and exhaustive, so that exactly one of them will be true whenever the statement is executed. The effect of such a statement is the same as that of a familiar **if**-statement.

Listing 1.4. Discriminant of a quadratic equation

```
1   active proctype P() {
2       int a = 1, b = -4, c = 4;
3       int disc;
4       disc = b * b - 4 * a * c;
5       if
6       :: disc < 0 ->
7           printf("disc = %d: no real roots\n", disc)
8       :: disc == 0 ->
9           printf("disc = %d: duplicate real roots\n", disc)
10      :: disc > 0 ->
11          printf("disc = %d: two real roots\n", disc)
12      fi
13  }
```

An **if**-statement starts with the reserved word **if** and ends with the reserved word **fi** (**if** spelled backward). In between are one or more *alternatives*, each consisting of a double colon, a statement called a *guard*, an arrow, and a sequence of statements.[6] (Note that no semicolon is required before a double colon or the **fi** because the semicolon is a separator, not a terminator.)

The execution of an **if**-statement begins with the evaluation of the guards; if at least one evaluates to true, the sequence of statements following the arrow corresponding to one of the true guards is executed. When those statements have been executed, the **if**-statement terminates.

Listing 1.5 shows a program for computing the number of days in a month. Compound boolean expressions are used for each guard. The example also shows the **else** guard whose meaning is: if and only if *all* the other guards evaluate to false, the statements following the **else** will be executed.

Listing 1.5. Number of days in a month

```
1   active proctype P() {
2     byte days;
3     byte month = 2;
4     int year = 2000;
5     if
6     :: month == 1 || month == 3 || month == 5 ||
7        month == 7 || month == 8 || month == 10 ||
8        month == 12 ->
9          days = 31
10    :: month == 4 || month == 6 || month == 9 ||
11       month == 11 ->
12         days = 30
13    :: month == 2 && year % 4 == 0 && /* Leap year */
14       (year % 100 != 0 || year % 400 == 0) ->
15         days = 29
16    :: else ->
17         days = 28
18    fi;
19    printf("month = %d, year = %d, days = %d\n",
20            month, year, days)
21  }
```

---

[6] In *SMC* an alternative is called an *option sequence*, but I prefer the former term.

> # Warning
>
> The **else** guard is not the same as a guard consisting of the constant **true**. The latter can *always* be selected even if there are other guards that evaluate to true, while the former is only selected if all other guards evaluate to false.

The next example shows how nondeterminism works. When computing the maximum of two values, it does not matter which is chosen if the two values are equal (Listing 1.6). If two or more guards evaluate to true, the statements associated with either may be executed. In the example, we have used an additional variable, branch, to record which alternative is taken. Run the program a few times and you will see that both values can be printed. This demonstrates the concept of random simulation: Whenever a nondeterministic choice exists, SPIN randomly chooses one of them.

Finally, it is possible that all alternatives could be false. In that case the process blocks until some guard evaluates to true, which can only happen in a concurrent program with more than one process (Chapter 3).

The sequence of statements following a guard can be empty, in which case control leaves the **if**-statement after evaluating the guard. If you are bothered by the empty sequence, you can use **skip**, which is syntactic sugar for a statement (actually, an expression) that always evaluates to true like **true** or (1).

Listing 1.6. Maximum of two values

```
1  active proctype P() {
2    int a = 5, b = 5;
3    int max;
4    int branch;
5    if
6    :: a >= b -> max = a; branch = 1
7    :: b >= a -> max = b; branch = 2
8    fi;
9    printf("The maximum of %d and %d = %d by branch %d\n",
10      a, b, max, branch)
11 }
```

Advanced: Arrows as separators

The arrow symbol is syntactic sugar for a semicolon. Guards are simply PROMELA statements with no special syntax, so, for example, the **if**-statement in Listing 1.4 is equivalent to one written as:

```
if
:: disc < 0 ; printf(...)
:: disc == 0 ; printf(...)
:: disc > 0 ; printf(...)
fi
```

The arrow syntax is preferred because it emphasizes the role of the guard in deciding which alternative to execute.

1.6.1 Conditional expressions*

A conditional expression enables you to obtain a value that depends on the result of evaluating a boolean expression:[7]

```
max = (a > b -> a : b)
```

The variable max is assigned the value of a if a > b; otherwise, it is assigned the value of b. The syntax is different from that in C-like languages: An arrow is used instead of a question mark to separate the condition from the two expressions.

Warning

A conditional expression *must* be contained within parentheses. It is a syntax error to write:
```
max = a > b -> a : b
```

In Listing 1.5, we could slightly simplify the computation of the number of days in February by using a conditional expression:

```
:: month == 2 && year % 4 == 0 ->
     days = (year % 100 != 0 || year % 400 == 0 ->
             29 : 28)
```

Note the difference between the two arrows: the first arrow separates the guard from the assignment statement, while the second arrow is used in the conditional expression.

The semantics of conditional expressions is different from that of **if**-statements. An assignment statement like

---

[7] In the *man* pages a conditional expression is called cond_expr.

```
max = (a > b -> a : b)
```

is an atomic statement, while the the **if**-statement

```
if
:: a > b -> max = a
:: else  -> max = b
fi
```

is not, and interleaving is possible between the guard and the following assignment statement.

1.7 Repetitive statements

There is one repetitive statement in PROMELA, the **do**-statement. The program in Listing 1.7 computes the greatest common denominator (GCD) of two values of type **int** by repeated subtraction of the smaller from the larger. The syntax of the **do**-statement is the same as that of the **if**-statement, except that the keywords are **do** and **od**. The semantics is similar, consisting of the evaluation of the guards, followed by the execution of the sequence of statements following one of the true guards. For a **do**-statement, completion of the sequence of statements causes the execution to return to the beginning of the **do**-statement and the evaluation of the guards is begun again.

Listing 1.7. Greatest common denominator

```
1   active proctype P() {
2     int x = 15, y = 20;
3     int a = x, b = y;
4     do
5     :: a > b -> a = a - b
6     :: b > a -> b = b - a
7     :: a == b -> break
8     od;
9     printf("The GCD of %d and %d = %d\n", x, y, a)
10  }
```

Termination of a loop is accomplished by **break**, which is not a statement but rather an indication that control passes from the current location to the statement following the **od**.

1.7.1 Counting loops

Unfortunately, there are no counting loops in PROMELA similar to the for-statements of C-like languages. The program in Listing 1.8 shows how to implement a counting loop. The control variable i is declared and initialized. One alternative of the **do**-statement (line 7) checks if the value of i is greater than the upper limit N, and if so executes a **break**. Otherwise (**else**), the body of the loop is executed and the control variable incremented (lines 8–10).

Listing 1.8. A counting loop

```
1   #define N 10
2
3   active proctype P() {
4      int sum = 0;
5      byte i = 1;
6      do
7      :: i > N -> break
8      :: else ->
9             sum = sum + i;
10            i++
11     od;
12     printf("The sum of the first %d numbers = %d\n", N, sum)
13  }
```

> ## Warning
>
> Do not forget the **else** in a counting loop! It is not an error of syntax to omit the **else** and so no error message will result. SPIN will nondeterministically choose to execute one of the alternatives whose guard evaluates to true (if any), and the results may be unexpected.

PROMELA contains a macro facility that can be used to make programs more readable (Section 6.3.2). Macros can be written to simulate the control statements of more familiar languages. Personally, I prefer to use PROMELA's guarded-commands syntax, except in the case of of counting loops. The program in Listing 1.9 shows how to implement the counting loop using a macro to simulate a for-statement. The **for** macro takes three parameters: the control variable, and the lower and upper limits of the loop. The **rof** macro at the end of the loop takes the control variable as a parameter. The text of these macros is contained in a file for.h which must be **include**'d in the program. Be sure that this file is in the same directory as your program. (The definition of these macros is given in Section 6.3.2.)

Listing 1.9. Counting with a for-loop macro

```
1   #include "for.h"
2   #define N 10
3
4   active proctype P() {
5      int sum = 0;
6      for (i, 1, N)
7         sum = sum + i
8      rof (i);
9      printf("The sum of the first %d numbers = %d\n", N, sum)
10  }
```

Warning

This macro declares the loop variable i, but does not create a new scope as in JAVA. If you use it more than once with the same variable, you will get an error message that the variable is multiply declared, although no harm is done and you can ignore the message. Alternatively, modify the macro to remove the declaration and declare the variable yourself.

1.8 Jump statements*

PROMELA contains a **goto**-statement that causes control to jump to a label, which is an identifier followed by a (single) colon. **goto** can be used instead of **break** to exit a loop:

```
    do
    :: i > N -> goto exitloop
    :: else -> ...
    od;
exitloop:
    printf(...);
```

though normally the **break** is preferred since it is more structured and doesn't require a label. See Section 8.1 for a reasonable use of the **goto**-statement.

Warning

There is no control point at the beginning of an alternative in an **if**- or **do**-statement, so it is a syntax error to place a label in front of a guard. Instead, there is a "joint" control point for all alternatives at the beginning of the statement.

Here is an example showing how a label must be attached to the entire **do**-statement and not to a single alternative:

```
start:
    do
    :: wantP ->
        if
        :: wantQ -> goto start
        :: else -> skip
        fi
    :: else ->
        ...
    od
```

Warning

Labels in PROMELA are not used only as targets of jump statements; they are also used in correctness specifications. See Sections 4.7.2 and 10.4.

2

Verification of Sequential Programs

Although SPIN is designed for verifying models of concurrent and distributed systems, we will introduce verification within the elementary context
of sequential programs. This chapter shows how to express correctness specifications using assertions and describes the procedure for carrying out a verification in SPIN.

2.1 Assertions

A *state* of a program is a set of values of its variables and location counters. For example, a state of the program in Listing 1.1 is a triple such as
(123, 321, 8), where the first element is the value of the variable value,
the second is the value of reversed, and the third shows that the location
counter is before the **printf** statement in line 8.

A *computation* of a program is a sequence of states beginning with an
initial state and continuing with the states that occur as each statement is
executed. There is only one computation for the program in Listing 1.1:

(123, 0, 4) -> (123, 321, 8) -> (123, 321, 9)

The *state space* of a program is the set of states that can *possibly* occur
during a computation.[1] In model checking the state space of a program is
generated in order to search for a counterexample – if one exists – to the
correctness specifications. This section shows how to use *assertions* to express
correctness specifications.

Assertions can be placed between any two statements of a program and
the model checker will evaluate the assertions as part of its search of the state
space. If, during the search, it finds a computation leading to a false assertion,

---

[1] Section 4.3 elaborates on the meaning of *possibly* in this context.

either the program is incorrect, or the assertion does not properly express a correctness property that holds for the program.

Listing 2.1 shows a program for integer division that works by repeatedly subtracting the divisor from the dividend until what remains is less than the divisor. We have added assertions to the program. The first assertion (line 6) is the *precondition*, an assertion that specifies what must be true in the initial state. Here the precondition states that the dividend is nonnegative and that the divisor is positive. The *postcondition* (lines 20–21) specifies what must be true in any final state of the program. The first line claims that the remainder is nonnegative and less than the divisor, and the second claims that the expected relation holds among the four quantities.

Listing 2.1. Integer division

```
1   active proctype P() {
2     int dividend = 15;
3     int divisor = 4;
4     int quotient, remainder;
5
6     assert (dividend >= 0 && divisor > 0);
7
8     quotient = 0;
9     remainder = dividend;
10    do
11    :: remainder >= divisor ->
12        quotient++;
13        remainder = remainder - divisor
14    :: else ->
15        break
16    od;
17    printf("%d divided by %d = %d, remainder = %d\n",
18        dividend, divisor, quotient, remainder);
19
20    assert (0 <= remainder && remainder < divisor);
21    assert (dividend == quotient * divisor + remainder)
22  }
```

Assertions are statements consisting of the keyword **assert** followed by an expression. When an **assert** statement is executed during a simulation, the expression is evaluated. If it is true, execution proceeds normally to the next statement; if it is false, the program terminates with an error message.

Run a random simulation for this program; it will terminate normally with no error messages, printing:

```
15 divided by 4 = 3, remainder = 3
```

Now, change the initial value of the variable dividend to 16 (line 2), change the guard remainder >= divisor to remainder > divisor (line 11), and re-run the simulation. The assertion in line 20 will evaluate to false and the program will terminate with the error message:

```
spin: line  20 "divide-error.pml", Error: assertion violated
spin: text of failed assertion:
   assert(((0<=remainder)&&(remainder<divisor)))
```

The error message identifies the assertion that evaluated to false. Using the data displayed in JSPIN or running SPIN from the command line with the argument -l will quickly show that the assertion is evaluated when both remainder and divisor equal 4, so that remainder < divisor is false.

Listing 2.2 shows another program for integer division. In addition to the precondition and postcondition, we have added an assertion within the loop (lines 11–12); this assertion is evaluated each time the first alternative of the do-statement (lines 9–21) is executed. An assertion within a loop is called an *invariant* of the loop because it must remain true as long as the loop body continues to be executed.

Run a verification (as described in the next section) and show that the program is correct.

Advanced: Preconditions in Promela models

Preconditions have little meaning when models are verified in SPIN. They are intended to specify conditions on the input to a program, but PROMELA models rarely, if ever, have input. Instead, initial values are given that trivially satisfy the precondition, as shown in the program in Listing 2.1. In a real system any input to the system will be received in a register or memory cell of finite size, so it can be modeled by PROMELA statements that nondeterministically choose values from a limited range (Section 4.6). Postconditions are more meaningful – for models that are intended to terminate – because there may be many different computations that can terminate, and it makes sense to specify properties of final states.

Listing 2.2. Another program for integer division

```
1   active proctype P() {
2     int dividend = 15, divisor = 4;
3     int quotient = 0, remainder = 0;
4     int n = dividend;
5
6     assert (dividend >= 0 && divisor > 0);
7
8     do
9     :: n != 0 ->
10
11      assert (dividend == quotient * divisor + remainder + n);
12      assert (0 <= remainder && remainder < divisor);
13
14        if
15        :: remainder + 1 == divisor ->
16            quotient++;
17            remainder = 0
18        :: else ->
19            remainder++
20        fi;
21        n--
22    :: else ->
23        break
24    od;
25    printf("%d divided by %d = %d, remainder = %d\n",
26        dividend, divisor, quotient, remainder);
27
28    assert (0 <= remainder && remainder < divisor);
29    assert (dividend == quotient * divisor + remainder)
30  }
```

Advanced: Deductive verification

An alternative approach to verification is *deduction*. A formal semantics is defined for program constructs and then a formal logic with axioms and inference rules is used to deduce that a program satisfies correctness specifications, expressed, for example, as assertions. The advantage of deductive verification is that it is not limited by the size of the state space because the deduction is done on symbolic formulas; the disadvantage is that it is less amenable to automation and requires mathematical ingenuity.

A deductive verification of the program in Listing 2.2 is given in Section B.4 of *PCDP*; it was partially automated using the verification capabilities of the SPARK system [3].

For an overview of deductive verification, see Chapter 9 of *MLCS*; an advanced textbook is [1].

2.2 Verifying a program in SPIN

Consider the program in Listing 2.3 that has an error in the second alternative (line 5). When a equals b a random simulation is just as likely to take the first alternative of the **if**-statement as the second. In fact, even if we run the simulation repeatedly, it is possible – although unlikely – that the same alternative will always be taken. In other words, no amount of simulation can ever verify that the postcondition is true, because it may become true if one alternative is taken, while it is falsified in the other alternative.

Listing 2.3. Maximum with an error

```
1  active proctype P() {
2         int a = 5, b = 5, max;
3         if
4         :: a >= b -> max = a;
5         :: b >= a -> max = b+1;
6         fi;
7         assert (a >= b -> max == a : max == b)
8  }
```

The only way to verify that a program is correct is to systematically check that the correctness specifications hold in *all possible computations*, and that is what model checkers like SPIN are designed to do.

In a deterministic program (with no input), there is only one possible computation, so a single random simulation will suffice to demonstrate the correctness of a program. For a concurrent or nondeterministic program, checking all possible computations involves executing the program and backtracking over each choice of the next statement to execute. One of the ways that SPIN achieves efficiency is by generating an optimized program called a *verifier* for each PROMELA model. Verification in SPIN is a three-step process (Figure 2.1):

- Generate the verifier from the PROMELA source code.
  The verifier is a program written in C.
- Compile the verifier using a C compiler.
- Execute the verifier. The result of the execution of the verifier is a report that *all* computations are correct or else that *some* computation contains an error. (The *Trail* shown in the figure is explained in the next section.)

Fortunately, there is no need to examine the C source code of the verifier; you simply perform these three steps within a script, or use JSPIN, which invokes SPIN, the C compiler and the compiled verifier.

Fig. 2.1. The architecture of SPIN

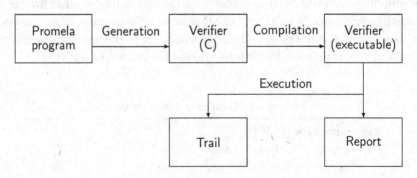

jSpin

Select Verify. The commands that are executed are listed in the message pane. The report of the verifier is displayed in the right pane.

Command line

Run SPIN with the argument -a to generate the verifier source code:

```
spin -a max.pml
```

Check your directory; you should find files pan.* including pan.c, which contains the source code of the main program. (The file name pan is historical and is derived from *protocol analyzer*.) The next step is to compile this file; for the gcc compiler the command is:

```
gcc -o pan pan.c
```

Finally, run the verifier:

```
pan
```

You may need to enter this command as ./pan or .\pan.

Verify the program in Listing 1.6 for the maximum of two numbers; you should get errors = 0. (For now, you can ignore the rest of the output.)

Next, verify the program in Listing 2.3 that contains an error; the report will be:

```
pan: assertion violated
    ( ((a>=b)) ? ((max==a)) : ((max==b)) ) (at depth 0)
pan: wrote max1.pml.trail
(Spin Version 4.2.8 -- 6 January 2007)
Warning: Search not completed
    ...
State-vector 24 byte, depth reached 2, errors: 1
    ...
```

SPIN does not bother to search the entire state space; instead, it stops as soon as one assertion is violated because the existence of one counterexample is usually sufficient to locate an error in the program or the correctness specifications.

Advanced: Continuing past the first error

The argument -e to pan causes trails for all errors to be created.
The argument -cN causes the verifier to stop at the Nth error rather than the first, while the argument -c0 requests the verifier to ignore all errors and not to generate a trail file.

2.2.1 Guided simulation

You may hope that your first attempt at verifying a model will succeed; however, this is unrealistically optimistic! Almost invariably it takes a long time to understand the interactions among components of the model, and between the model and its correctness specifications, in order to achieve a successful verification. Thus, a primary task of a model checker is to assist the systems engineer in understanding why a verification has failed.

SPIN supports the analysis of failed verifications by maintaining internal data structures during its search of the state space; these are used to reconstruct a computation that leads to an error. The data required for reconstructing a computation are written into a file called a *trail*. (The name of the file is the same as that of the PROMELA source code file with the additional extension .trail.) The trail file is not intended to be read; rather, it is used to reconstruct a computation by running SPIN in *guided simulation mode*.

---

jSpin

After running a verification that has reported errors, select Trail .

Command line

After running a verification that has reported errors, run SPIN again with the -t argument:

```
spin -t max.pml
```

An examination of the guided simulation for the program in Listing 2.3 will show that the bad computation actually occurs when the alternative with the mistake (line 5) is executed:

```
Starting P with pid 0
    0:    proc  - (:root:) creates proc  0 (P)
    0 P    3    b>=a
    0 P    5    max = (b+1)
```

As a check of your understanding of assertions, write the postcondition for the program in Listing 1.7 that computes the greatest common denominator of two integer numbers; verify that the program is correct.

2.2.2 Displaying a computation

When examining a computation produced by a random or guided simulation, we need more than the output that results from the print statements.

We need to examine the sequence of statements executed, as well as the state of the computation – the values of the variables and the location counters – after executing each statement. SPIN can print any subset of the following data:

- The statements executed by the processes;
- The values of the global variables;
- The values of the local variables;
- Send instructions executed on a channel (see Chapter 7);
- Receive instructions executed on a channel (see Chapter 7).

To select which data to display:

jSpin

Select Options / Common and select the data you want displayed. It is simplest to check all of them (Set all).

The states are displayed in tabular form in the right pane with a separate entry for each state. An entry contains the statement executed, the process it came from, and the values of the variables in the program.

JSPIN has many options for customizing the display of data during a simulation. You can interactively choose to exclude some variables or statements from the display by entering their identifiers in the text areas that pop up after selecting Output / Exclude variables or Output / Exclude statements.

The width of the fields used for displaying the values of the variables can be specified by selecting Output / Variable width.

To maximize the right pane, select Output / Maximize (alt-M).

Command line

The following arguments cause SPIN to display the data described above during a simulation: -p (statements), -g (globals), -l (locals), -s (send), -r (receive).

Each item of data is displayed on a separate line. You can redirect the output into a file and then examine the data using an editor.

3

Concurrency

Many computers are used in *embedded systems*, which are composed of hardware, software, sensors, controllers and displays, and which are intended to be run indefinitely and without continuous supervision. One only has to think of airplanes, medical monitors, and cell phone networks to appreciate the complexity of embedded systems. Invariably, these systems contain several *processes* that must sample sensors and perform computations at roughly the same time; for example, a medical monitor samples heart rate, blood pressure, and temperature, and determines if they are within a predetermined range. Programming for multiprocess systems is called *concurrent programming*.

Frequently, embedded systems contain several *processors*; microprocessors have become so inexpensive that it is feasible to devote a separate processor to each subsystem. Furthermore, many systems like cell phone networks are by nature geographically dispersed, relying on communications networks for passing data between processors. Programming for such systems is called *distributed programming*.

SPIN supports modeling of both concurrent and distributed systems. This chapter is the first of several on writing and verifying concurrent programs; in Chapter 7 we discuss the use of channels to model distributed systems.

3.1 Interleaving

Consider the program in Listing 3.1 with two processes, P and Q. A computation of the program can be displayed in a table with one line for each state that forms the computation. The top line is the initial state. The entry for a state shows the values of the variables and the statement that will be

Listing 3.1. Interleaving statements

```
1  byte  n = 0;
2
3  active proctype P() {
4    n = 1;
5    printf("Process P, n = %d\n", n)
6  }
7
8  active proctype Q() {
9    n = 2;
10   printf("Process Q, n = %d\n", n)
11 }
```

executed next, together with the process in which the statement is declared. Here is the table for one computation of the program in Listing 3.1:[1]

Process	Statement	n	Output
P	n = 1	0	
P	printf(P)	1	
Q	n = 2	1	P, n = 1
Q	printf(Q)	2	
			Q, n = 2

In the initial state, the first statement executed is n = 1 from process P and that leads to the next state in which the value of n is 1; process P prints this value. Then process Q assigns the value 2 to n and prints the value. The program terminates in a state with the value 2 in the global variable n.

However, this is not the only possible computation of the program. There are six possible computations of the program:

1	2	3	4	5	6
n = 1	n = 1	n = 1	n = 2	n = 2	n = 2
printf(P)	n = 2	n = 2	printf(Q)	n = 1	n = 1
n = 2	printf(P)	printf(Q)	n = 1	printf(Q)	printf(P)
printf(Q)	printf(Q)	printf(P)	printf(P)	printf(P)	printf(Q)

---

[1] To save space, the **printf** statements have been abbreviated.

These computations correspond to the following outputs:

```
Process P, n = 1     Process P, n = 2     Process Q, n = 2
Process Q, n = 2     Process Q, n = 2     Process P, n = 1


Process Q, n = 2     Process Q, n = 1     Process P, n = 1
Process P, n = 1     Process P, n = 1     Process Q, n = 1
```

We say that the computations of a program are obtained by *arbitrarily interleaving* of the statements of the processes. If each process p_i were run by itself, a computation of the process would be a sequence of states $(s_i^0, s_i^1, s_i^2, \ldots)$, where state s_i^{j+1} follows state s_i^j if and only if it is obtained by executing the statement at the location counter of p_i in s_i^j.

Consider now a computation obtained by running all processes concurrently. It is a sequence of states $(s^0, s^1, s^2, \ldots)$, where s^{j+1} follows state s^j if and only if it is obtained by executing the statement at the location counter of *some* process in s^j. The word "interleaving" is intended to represent this image of "selecting" a statement from the possible computations of the individual processes and "merging" then into a computation of all the processes of the system.

For the program in Listing 3.1, a state is a triple consisting of the value of n and the location counters of processes P and Q. The computation obtained by executing the processes by themselves can be represented as

```
(0, 4, -) -> (1, 5, -) -> (1, 6, -)
```

for process P, and

```
(0, -, 9) -> (2, -, 10) -> (2, -, 11)
```

for process Q. The third computation above is obtained by interleaving the two separate computations:

```
(0, 4, 9)    ->    "select" from P
(1, 5, 9)    ->    "select" from Q
(2, 5, 10)   ->    "select" from Q
(2, 5, 11)   ->    "select" from P
(2, 6, 11)
```

3.1.1 Displaying a computation

When SPIN simulates a program it creates *one* computation by interleaving the statements of all the processes. SPIN writes a description of the computation on standard output; JSPIN formats this description to make it easier to understand.

jSpin

The output of a simulation is displayed in the right pane; here is the output for computation 4 from page 30:

```
Process Q, n = 2
Process P, n = 1
2 processes created
```

A tabular format of the states of the computation can be displayed. Select Options / Common / Set all / OK (see Section 2.2.2). Here is the table for computation 1:

```
0 P    4   n = 1
Process Statement         n
0 P    5   printf('Proces 1
1 Q    9   n = 2            1
1 Q   10   printf('Proces 2
```

The first columns contain the process ID (number) and name; this is followed by the line number and source code of the statement executed (truncated if necessary), and then the values of the variables.

Command line

When SPIN writes the output of a concurrent program, it automatic indents **printf** statements so that it is easy to see which statement comes from which process. The output for computation 4 (page 30) is:

```
      Process Q, n = 2
    Process P, n = 1
  2 processes created
```

and the output from computation 6 is:

```
    Process P, n = 1
      Process Q, n = 1
  2 processes created
```

The argument -T turns off the automatic indentation.

Section 2.2.2 listed the arguments that enable the display of the statements that are executed and the values of the variables. Here is the output (edited to fit on the page) that is obtained by running with the arguments -p -g. There is a line for each statement executed and a line that displays the value of the variable n *when it changes*.

```
Starting P with pid 0
0: proc  - (:root:) creates proc  0 (P)
Starting Q with pid 1
0: proc  - (:root:) creates proc  1 (Q)
1: proc  1 (Q) line   9 (state 1) [n = 2]
              n = 2
      Process Q, n = 2
2: proc  1 (Q) line  10 (state 2) [printf(Q)]
2: proc  1 (Q)              terminates
3: proc  0 (P) line   4 (state 1) [n = 1]
              n = 1
      Process P, n = 1
4: proc  0 (P) line   5 (state 2) [printf(Q)]
4: proc  0 (P)              terminates
2 processes created
```

3.2 Atomicity

Statements in PROMELA are *atomic*. At each step, the statement pointed to by
the location counter of some (arbitrary) process is executed in its entirety. So,
for example, in Listing 3.1 it is not possible for the assignment statements to
overlap in a way that causes n to receives some value other than 1 or 2.

Warning

Expressions in PROMELA are *statements*.

In an **if**- or **do**-statement it is possible for interleaving to occur
between the evaluation of the expression (statement) that is the
guard and the execution of the statement after the guard.

In the following example, assume that a is a global variable; you *cannot*
infer that division by zero is impossible:

```
if
:: a != 0 ->
      c = b / a
:: else ->
      c = b
fi
```

Between the evaluation of the guard a != 0 and the execution of the assignment statement c = b / a, some other process might have assigned zero to a. In Section 4.4 we will discuss ways of executing the statements of a sequence atomically, and in Section 3.4 we show how to model hardware at a level lower than a complete expression.

3.3 Interactive simulation

When there are two or more nontrivial processes in a PROMELA program, the number of computations becomes extremely large because every possible interleaving gives rise to a computation. Random simulation tells us almost nothing about the program, except that it works for a few computations. Therefore, verification is essential when one deals with concurrent programs. Verifications are quite likely to find counterexamples and these computations can be displayed as described in Section 2.2.1. However, it is also useful to examine a computation step by step and to manually "select" the next instruction to be executed; in other words, to create a specific interleaving.

With *interactive simulation* a specific computation can be constructed. Before each step that has a *choice point* – either because of nondeterminism within a single process or when a choice of the next statement to execute can be made from several processes – you are presented with the various choices and can interactively choose which one to execute. To run an interactive simulation:

jSpin

Select Interactive. The set of choices at each step is displayed in a popup window:

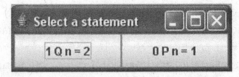

Click on the one you wish to execute. The selections are prefixed by the process ID and name, as the same source statement may appear in several processes. At any time you can close the window to terminate the simulation.

To work with the keyboard: Tab moves between the choices and Space selects the currently highlighted choice. Esc terminates the simulation.

Command line

Execute SPIN with the argument -i. Before each step you will be presented with a set of choices:

```
Select a statement
  choice 1: proc  1 (Q) line   9 (state 1) [n = 2]
  choice 2: proc  0 (P) line   4 (state 1) [n = 1]
Select [1-2]:
```

Enter the number of the choice you wish to execute or q to terminate the interactive simulation.

Warning

The numbering may not start at one.

Be sure to enter the *choice number* and not the *line number*.

Some of the choices may not be executable. For example, if the value of x is 1 and the statement to be executed is a guard x > 1, the choice will be marked as unexecutable and you cannot select it.

3.4 Interference between processes

The challenge of writing concurrent programs comes not from interleaving as such, but rather from interference between processes that can cause truly bizarre errors. Consider the program in Listing 3.2 that increments the global variable n in each of two processes. Its value is copied into the local variables temp when the add operations are performed, and the result is copied back to the global variable in a separate assignment statement. (This models a CPU that performs computation in registers as explained in more detail at the end of this section.) Between the statements of process P on lines 5 and 6 it is possible to interleave statements from process Q, and similarly for process Q. Such interleaving would not be possible if the computation were performed in a single atomic statement n = n + 1.

Clearly, we expect that incrementing the variable n twice will cause its final value to be 2, whatever the order in which the increment instructions are executed. Surprisingly, this is not true, as can be seen by the computation in Figure 3.1, in which the final value is 1.[2] This results from interference

---

[2] Since the variable temp is used in both processes, we prefix the variable name by its process name to resolve the ambiguity.

Listing 3.2. Interference between two processes

```
1  byte  n = 0;
2
3  active proctype P() {
4    byte temp;
5    temp = n + 1;
6    n = temp;
7    printf("Process P, n = %d\n", n)
8  }
9
10 active proctype Q() {
11   byte temp;
12   temp = n + 1;
13   n = temp;
14   printf("Process Q, n = %d\n", n)
15 }
```

between the two processes. Both copy the same initial value, and the updated value from one process is overwritten by the updated value from the second process. Run a random simulation of the program several times until you get a computation in which 1 is printed twice. To ensure that you understand how the computation is obtained, create it by interactive simulation.

Fig. 3.1. Perfect interleaving

Process	Statement	n	P:temp	Q:temp	Output
P	temp = n + 1	0	0	0	
Q	temp = n + 1	0	1	0	
P	n = temp	0	1	1	
Q	n = temp	1	1	1	
P	**printf**(P)	1	1	1	
Q	**printf**(Q)	1	1	1	P, n = 1
					Q, n = 1

Advanced: Modeling a CPU with registers

This program is a simple model of a CPU that performs computation in registers:

```
load    R1, n
add     R1, #1
store   R1, n
```

In the PROMELA program the variable n represents a memory cell and the variables temp represent the register. In a multiprocess system each process has its own copy of the contents of the registers, which is loaded into the CPU registers and saved in memory during a context switch. We have modeled the computation in two statements rather than three, since the add operation is not visible outside the process, so there is no need to model it separately and it can be combined with either the load or the store operation. Alternatively, we could have used three statements and let the SPIN optimization called partial order reduction reduce the state space automatically (Section 10.2).

3.5 Sets of processes

In Listing 3.2 the two processes are identical except for their names. Instead of writing them separately, a set of identical processes can be declared (Listing 3.3). The number in brackets following the keyword **active** (line 3) indicates the number of processes to instantiate.

Listing 3.3. Instantiating two processes

```
1  byte   n = 0;
2
3  active [2] proctype P() {
4    byte temp;
5    temp = n + 1;
6    n = temp;
7    printf("Process P%d, n = %d\n", _pid, n)
8  }
```

How are we to distinguish between the processes? One way is to use the predefined variable **_pid**, which is of a separate type **pid** but actually similar to **byte**. Each time that a process is instantiated, it is assigned a *process identifier* starting with zero. (The maximum number of processes in a SPIN model is 255.) In the program in Listing 3.3, the value of **_pid** is printed so that we can distinguish between the two processes on output (line 7).

An alternate way of instantiating processes from a **proctype** is to use the **run** operator (Listing 3.4). The keyword **run** is followed by the name of a *process type* (lines 13–14), which is indicated by **proctype** without the keyword **active** (line 3); this causes a process of that type to be instantiated. **run** is used to supply initial values to a process: the formal parameters are declared in the process type and are local variables initialized with the values of the actual parameters.

Processes in PROMELA are usually instantiated in a process called **init**, which – if it exists – is always the first process activated and thus the value of **_pid** in this process is 0. In Listing 3.4, the processes are instantiated in an **init** process where they are passed an explicit identifier id, as well as an additional value incr that is used in the assignment statements. The initialization of the global variable has also been moved to the **init** process (line 11), though this would normally be done only for non-trivial initialization code such as the nondeterministic selection of a value (Section 4.6).

By convention, **run** statements are enclosed in an **atomic** sequence to ensure that all processes are instantiated before any of them begins execution (lines 12–15). The meaning of **atomic** will be explained in the next section.

Warning

The formal parameters of a **proctype** are separated with semicolons, not commas.

Advanced: The run operator

run is an *operator*, so **run** P() is an expression, not a statement, and it returns a value: the process ID of the process that is instantiated, or zero if the maximum number of processes (255) have already been instantiated.

3.6 Interference revisited

The use of **init** enables us to write a fascinating program for demonstrating interference. The program in Listing 3.5 contains two processes, each of which increments the global variable n ten times.

Listing 3.4. The **init** process

```
1   byte  n;
2
3   proctype P(byte id; byte incr) {
4     byte temp;
5     temp = n + incr;
6     n = temp;
7     printf("Process P%d, n = %d\n", id, n)
8   }
9
10  init {
11    n = 0;
12    atomic {
13      run P(1, 10);
14      run P(2, 15)
15    }
16  }
```

We wish to print the final value of n after the two processes have completed executing their statements, so we need some way to force process **init** to wait for the completion of the other two. This can be done by using the predefined variable **_nr_pr** whose value is the number of processes currently active. The statement in line 17 consisting just of the expression

(**_nr_pr** == 1)

causes process **init** to be blocked until the expression evaluates to true, which occurs when the number of active processes is equal to 1, namely, the process **init** itself. (The use of expressions for blocking execution will be discussed in Section 4.2.)

Consider now two computations. In the first the computation is performed without interference: One process executes *all* its statements in sequence, followed by *all* the statements of the second process. It is easy to see that the final value of n is 20. The second computation is performed by "perfect" interleaving: The computation is created by *alternately* "selecting" one statement from each process, generalizing the computation shown in Figure 3.1. It is not difficult to see that each pair of updates of the variable n increments its value by 1, and the final value is 10.

Intuitively, it seems as if "perfect" interleaving represents the maximum "amount of interference" possible, and for many years I taught that the final

Listing 3.5. Counting with interference

```
1   #include "for.h"
2   byte  n = 0;
3
4   proctype P() {
5     byte temp;
6     for (i, 1, 10)
7       temp = n + 1;
8       n = temp
9     rof (i)
10  }
11
12  init {
13    atomic {
14      run P();
15      run P()
16    }
17    (_nr_pr == 1) ->
18        printf("The value is %d\n", n)
19  }
```

value of n must be between 10 and 20. It came somewhat of a shock when I discovered that the final value can be as low as 2 (see [6])! Try to find the computation yourself; if you can't, we will show in Section 3.8 how verification can be used to discover it.

3.7 Deterministic sequences of statements*

As noted in Section 3.2, each statement of PROMELA (including expressions) is executed atomically. Thus, n = n + 1 is executed atomically, so to model a CPU with an accumulator we wrote a program with local variables and two assignment statements (Listing 3.2).

To model atomic statements that are more complex than a single assignment statement, we can specify that a sequence of statements is to be executed atomically. There are two ways of creating atomic sequences of statements: **d_step** (short for deterministic step) and **atomic**. Listing 3.6 shows the use of **d_step** to ensure that the two statements in the processes in Listing 3.2 are executed atomically (lines 5–8, 14–17), resulting in a program that is equivalent to one with the two-statement sequences replaced by n = n + 1. The following computation shows that executing the program prints the expected result:

Process	Statement	n	P:temp	Q:temp	Output
P	temp = n + 1; n = temp	0	0	0	
Q	temp = n + 1; n = temp	1	1	0	
P	printf("P")	2	1	2	
Q	printf("Q")	2	1	2	P, n = 2
					Q, n = 2

In this example, **atomic** can be used instead of **d_step**. The difference between the two will be explained in Section 4.4.

Listing 3.6. Deterministic step

```
1  byte  n = 0;
2
3  active proctype P() {
4    byte temp;
5    d_step {
6      temp = n + 1;
7      n = temp
8    }
9    printf("Process P, n = %d\n", n)
10 }
11
12 active proctype Q() {
13   byte temp;
14   d_step {
15     temp = n + 1;
16     n = temp
17   }
18   printf("Process Q, n = %d\n", n)
19 }
```

There are many synchronization primitives such as *test-and-set* and *exchange* that are based upon the atomic execution of a sequence of statements. These are explained in Section 3.10 of *PCDP*, and implementations in PROMELA are given in the software archive for that book.

3.8 Verification with assertions

Consider again the program in Listing 3.5 that increments a global variable by 10 in each of two processes. We claimed that there is a computation whose output is 2. How can we check this? We can run random simulations until it occurs, and that is how I was first made aware of the existence of such a computation: A student in a computer lab executed the program again and again using a concurrency simulator and called me over when the output was 9, a result totally at odds with my intuition. Eventually, I discovered the principle behind the computation, as well as the fact that such a computation can result in an output of 2.

With SPIN the computation can be obtained automatically by adding the assertion

assert (n > 2)

at the end of the program and running a verification. You can be excused if this assertion looks weird: We want to prove that the variable n can have the value 2, but instead we assert that its value is *greater than* 2. What SPIN does is to search the state space looking for *counterexamples*, that is, computations that are in error. If the assertion given were n >= 2, SPIN would report a successful verification with no errors because, in fact, the final value of n really is greater than or equal to 2. By asserting the false formula n > 2, SPIN will find a computation in which n > 2 false, that is, a computation for which its negation n <= 2 is true.

Running a verification with SPIN results in the error message:

pan: assertion violated (n>2) (at depth 89)

As described in Section 2.2, a guided simulation can now be run with the trail in order to examine the computation that caused the assertion to be falsified. The following computation is taken with very little editing directly from the JSPIN display; to save space, the program was run with an upper limit of 5 for the loop:

Process	Statement		P(1):temp	P(2):temp	n
2 P	7	temp = n			
1 P	7	temp = n	0		
2 P	8	n = (temp+1)	0	0	
2 P	7	temp = n	0	0	1
2 P	8	n = (temp+1)	0	1	1
2 P	7	temp = n	0	1	2
2 P	8	n = (temp+1)	0	2	2
2 P	7	temp = n	0	2	3
2 P	8	n = (temp+1)	0	3	3
1 P	8	n = (temp+1)	0	3	4
2 P	7	temp = n	0	3	1
1 P	7	temp = n	0	1	1
1 P	8	n = (temp+1)	1	1	1
1 P	7	temp = n	1	1	2
1 P	8	n = (temp+1)	2	1	2
1 P	7	temp = n	2	1	3
1 P	8	n = (temp+1)	3	1	3
1 P	7	temp = n	3	1	4
1 P	8	n = (temp+1)	4	1	4
2 P	8	n = (temp+1)	4	1	5
0 :init	16	_nr_pr==1	4	1	2

The value of temp in P2 is reset to 1 and remains 1 so that a final addition
ignores the value 4 already set in n.

jSpin

The computation of a simulation will be displayed in the right pane.
Select Output / Save output to write the contents of the display to
a file which you can edit as necessary. For this display the width of
the variable fields was set to 10 and the loop variables i of the two
processes were excluded from the display, as were the statements
that access i. See Section 2.2.2 for instructions on how to do this.

Command line

The output of a simulation can be redirected to a file:

```
pan -t count-verif.pml > count-verif.out
```

3.9 The critical section problem

This section begins the presentation of the verification of correctness properties of concurrent systems. To that end we pose the *critical section problem*, which is the archetypal problem in concurrent programming. We will not attempt to give the motivation of this problem, nor a comprehensive set of solutions, as these can be found in textbooks on concurrency like *PCDP*. Let us just state the specification of the problem:

> A system consists of two or more concurrently executing processes. The statements of each process are divided into *critical* and *noncritical* sections that are repeatedly executed one after the other. A process may halt in its noncritical section, but not in its critical section. Design an algorithm for ensuring that the following specifications hold:
>
> **Mutual exclusion**
>> At most one process is executing its critical section at any time.
>
> **Absence of deadlock**
>> It is impossible to reach a state in which *some processes* are trying to enter their critical sections, but *no process* is successful.
>
> **Absence of starvation**
>> If *any process* is trying to execute its critical section, then eventually *that process* is successful.

The program in Listing 3.7 shows an attempt at solving the critical section problem for two processes. Each process executes a nonterminating **do**-statement (lines 4–9, 13–18), alternating between the critical and the noncritical sections which are represented by **printf** statements. The phrase "a process tries to execute its critical section" means that the process has finished executing its noncritical section and its location counter is at the following statement (lines 6, 15). Note that the possibility of halting in the noncritical section has not been modeled (see Section 5.9.2).

The variables wantP and wantQ are used to signal that a process is accessing its critical section; a process sets its variable to true before the critical section (lines 6, 15) and back to false afterwards (lines 8, 17). Of course, since a process never checks the value of the variable associated with the other process, it is trivial to find a computation in which they are both in their critical sections, indicated by both location counters pointing to the print statements representing the critical section (lines 7, 16). Thus the program in Listing 3.8 is trivially incorrect, but it serves to introduce the structure of a solution to the problem.

In a sequential program a postcondition must be true when the program terminates, and, similarly, an invariant must be true whenever the program

Listing 3.7. Incorrect solution for the critical section problem

```
1  bool wantP = false, wantQ = false;
2
3  active proctype P() {
4    do
5    :: printf("Noncritical section P\n");
6       wantP = true;
7       printf("Critical section P\n");
8       wantP = false
9    od
10 }
11
12 active proctype Q() {
13   do
14   :: printf("Noncritical section Q\n");
15      wantQ = true;
16      printf("Critical section Q\n");
17      wantQ = false
18   od
19 }
```

evaluates it. However, in a concurrent program, we generally need correctness specifications that consider the global state of *all* the processes in the
program. For example, to specify that two processes cannot be in their critical sections at the same time, the specification must refer to control points in
both processes.

One way of doing this is to introduce a new variable (`critical`) that is
not part of the algorithm but is only used for verification (Listing 3.8). Such
a variable is called a *ghost variable*. The variable is incremented before executing a critical section (lines 8, 20) and decremented afterwards (lines 11,
23); clearly, if there exists a state in some computation in which both location
counters are at the print statements representing the critical section (lines 9,
21), then in that state the value of `critical` is greater than one.[3]

Running a verification uncovers a state in which the value of the variable
`critical` is 2 when one of the **assert** statements is executed, indicating that
mutual exclusion has been violated:

---

[3] This property can also be specified and verified without ghost variables as shown
in Section 5.7.

Listing 3.8. Verifying mutual exclusion

```
1   bool wantP = false, wantQ = false;
2   byte critical = 0;
3
4   active proctype P() {
5     do
6     :: printf("Noncritical section P\n");
7        wantP = true;
8        critical++;
9        printf("Critical section P\n");
10       assert (critical <= 1);
11       critical--;
12       wantP = false
13    od
14  }
15
16  active proctype Q() {
17    do
18    :: printf("Noncritical section Q\n");
19       wantQ = true;
20       critical++;
21       printf("Critical section Q\n");
22       assert (critical <= 1);
23       critical--;
24       wantQ = false
25    od
26  }
```

```
spin: line  23 "cs.pml", Error: assertion violated
spin: text of failed assertion: assert((critical<=1))
#processes: 2
Process Statement          critical   wantP      wantQ
1 Q                         2          1          1
0 P                         2          1          1
```

In the next chapter we will explore how synchronization between processes can be achieved in order to solve the critical section problem.

4

Synchronization

PROMELA does not have synchronization primitives such as semaphores, locks, and monitors that you may have encountered. Instead, you model primitives by building on the concept of the *executability* of statements. The architecture of a computer system constrains the design of synchronization mechanisms: In this chapter, we present synchronization mechanisms appropriate for models of shared memory systems, while in Chapter 7 we will discuss channels that are used to model synchronization by communication in distributed systems that lack shared memory.

4.1 Synchronization by blocking

The program in Listing 3.8 that attempted to solve the critical section problem was trivially incorrect because, while each process set a variable indicating its intention to enter its critical section, these variables were not read by the other process. A simple-minded way to try to remedy this difficulty is to write a loop before the entry to the critical section, checking the value of the variable associated with the *other* process (Listing 4.1). This is called *busy-waiting* because the loops in lines 7–10 and 20–23 perform no useful computation; they just evaluate expressions repeatedly until they become true.

While busy-waiting is an acceptable model for some systems – for example, for a multiprocessor with a large number of processors that can afford to have some of them "waste" cycles waiting for an event to occur – normally, computer systems are based upon *blocking* a process so that its processor can be assigned to another process.

Synchronization by blocking will be familiar to anyone with experience in operating systems that implement *multitasking*, the sharing of a single processor among a set of processes. It is multitasking that enables us to perform

Listing 4.1. Synchronization by busy-waiting

```
 1  bool wantP = false, wantQ = false;
 2
 3  active proctype P() {
 4    do
 5    :: printf("Noncritical section P\n");
 6       wantP = true;
 7       do
 8       :: !wantQ -> break
 9       :: else -> skip
10       od;
11       printf("Critical section P\n");
12       wantP = false
13    od
14  }
15
16  active proctype Q() {
17    do
18    :: printf("Noncritical section Q\n");
19       wantQ = true;
20       do
21       :: !wantP -> break
22       :: else -> skip
23       od;
24       printf("Critical section Q\n");
25       wantQ = false
26    od
27  }
```

activities in parallel, like scrolling through one web page while another is being downloaded. Processes executing concurrently must be synchronized if they access common resources; for example, only one process may be allowed to update the display at any time. Synchronization in multitasking systems is implemented by having a process execute an operation that causes it to become blocked, thus enabling another process to run. Continuing our example, *if* one process is assigned permission to use a resource like the display, *then* other processes that need the display will block themselves until the first process releases it. This shows that blocking is frequently *conditional*.

In the program in Listing 4.1, we would like process P to block itself *until* wantQ becomes false and process Q to block itself *until* wantP becomes false.

We have already encountered a blocking statement in PROMELA, the **if**-statement. Recall (Section 1.6) that an **if**-statement contains a set of alternatives that start with expressions called guards.[1] An alternative is *executable* if its guard evaluates to **true** (or 1, which is the same). The choice of the alternative to execute is made nondeterministically among the executable alternatives. If no guards evaluate to true, the **if**-statement itself is not executable. Similarly, in a **do**-statement, if the guards of all alternatives evaluate to false, the statement is not executable and the process is blocked.

Let us replace the **do**-statements that implement busy-waiting in Listing 4.1 by **do**-statements with a single alternative that can block. In process P replace lines 7–10 by:

```
do
:: !wantQ -> break
od
```

and in process Q replace lines 20–23 by:

```
do
:: !wantP -> break
od
```

Consider now an attempt to execute the **do**-statement in process P. The guard !wantQ will be evaluated: if its value is true (because the value of the variable wantQ is false), the computation will execute the **break** and exit the **do**-statement. If, on the other hand, the guard !wantQ is false, the process is blocked at the **do**-statement.

To say that a process is blocked means that in simulation mode SPIN will not choose the next statement to execute from that process. In verification mode it means that SPIN will not continue the search for a counterexample from this state by looking for states that can be reached by executing a statement from the process. Hopefully, a subsequent execution of statements from other processes will *unblock* the blocked process, enabling it to continue executing in simulation mode, and in verification mode, enabling the verifier to search for states reachable by executing a statement from the process. If process P blocks because wantQ is true, eventually, process Q will execute line 25, setting wantQ to false and unblocking process P.

Check this behavior by running an interactive simulation of the program. Execute statements of the program until a state is reached in which P is

---

[1] Any statement, not just an expression, can be a guard, but expressions alone will be used in the following discussion.

blocked because wantQ is true; in this state you will not be allowed to choose to execute a statement from process P. Now choose to execute statements from Q until the statement wantQ = **false** is executed, enabling the execution of the a statement from P.

4.2 Executability of statements

> **Warning**
>
> The concept presented in this section is likely to be unfamiliar even to experienced programmers. Please read it carefully!

There is something rather strange about the construct:

```
do
:: !wantQ -> break
od
```

Either wantQ is false and the **break** causes the loop to be left, or it is true and the process blocks; when it is unblocked the process can leave the loop. In no case is there any "looping," so the **do**-statement is superfluous. In PROMELA it is possible to block on a simple statement, not just on a compound statement. Lines 7–10 in Listing 4.1 can be replaced by a single statement that is the expression !wantQ, and similarly, lines 20–23 by !wantP. An expression statement is *executable* if and only if it evaluates to true, in this case if the value of wantQ is false.

Listing 4.2 shows the program for the critical section problem written as it should be in PROMELA, with expressions alone used for blocking processes.[2] Again, we suggest that you run an interactive simulation of the program in order to experience the phenomenon of blocking on an expression.

The concept of executability holds for *every* statement in PROMELA. In the *man* page for each statement in PROMELA there is a section that specifies the conditions for the statement to be executable. Assignment statements and **printf** statements are always executable, so executability is primarily meaningful for expressions that can evaluate to true or false, including those that appear as guards in compound statements. The conditions for executability are also important in the definitions of channel operations (Chapter 7).

---

[2] This is the *third attempt* at solving the critical section problem in Chapter 3 of *PCDP*.

Listing 4.2. Synchronization with deadlock

```
1  bool wantP = false, wantQ = false;
2
3  active proctype P() {
4    do
5    :: printf("Noncritical section P\n");
6       wantP = true;
7       !wantQ;
8       printf("Critical section P\n");
9       wantP = false
10   od
11 }
12
13 active proctype Q() {
14   do
15   :: printf("Noncritical section Q\n");
16      wantQ = true;
17      !wantP;
18      printf("Critical section Q\n");
19      wantQ = false
20   od
21 }
```

4.3 State transition diagrams

Recall (Section 2.1) that a *state* of a program is a set of values of the variables and the location counters, and consider a program with two processes p and q that have s_p and s_q statements, respectively, and two variables x and y that range over v_x and v_y values, respectively. The number of possible states that can appear in computations of the program is

$$s_p \cdot s_q \cdot v_x \cdot v_y.$$

For example, the program in Listing 4.3 has $3 \cdot 3 \cdot 2 \cdot 2 = 36$ possible states.

However, not every possible state is *reachable* from the initial state during a computation of the program. In particular, a solution to the critical section problem is correct only if there are possible states that are *not* reachable, namely, states where the location counters of both processes are in their critical sections, thus falsifying the requirement of mutual exclusion.

Listing 4.3. Abbreviated solution for the critical section problem

```
1   bool wantP = false, wantQ = false;
2
3   active proctype P() {
4     do :: wantP = true;
5          !wantQ;
6          wantP = false
7     od
8   }
9
10  active proctype Q() {
11    do :: wantQ = true;
12         !wantP;
13         wantQ = false
14    od
15  }
```

In principle, the set S of reachable states of a program is easily constructed:

1. Let $S = \{s_0\}$, where s_0 is the initial state; mark s_0 as *unexplored*.
2. For each unexplored state $s \in S$, let t be a state that results from executing an executable statement in state s; if $t \notin S$, add t to S and mark it unexplored. If no such states exist, mark s as *explored*.
3. Terminate when all states in S are marked explored.

The reachable states of a concurrent program can be visualized as a connected directed graph called a *state transition diagram*. The nodes of the diagram are the reachable states and an edge exists from state s to state t if and only if there is a statement whose execution in s leads to t.

Figure 4.1 is the state transition diagram of the program in Listing 4.3.[3] Each node is labeled by the location counters for processes P and Q, followed by the values of the variables wantP and wantQ. To facilitate reading the diagram, the value of a location counter is given together with the source code at that control point.

The node that represents the initial state is at the top of the figure and the other nodes and the edges are constructed as described above. Most states have two outgoing edges because the next statement could be executed either

---

[3] The relation of Listing 4.3 to Listing 4.2 is explained at the end of this section.

Fig. 4.1. State diagram for the program in Listing 4.3

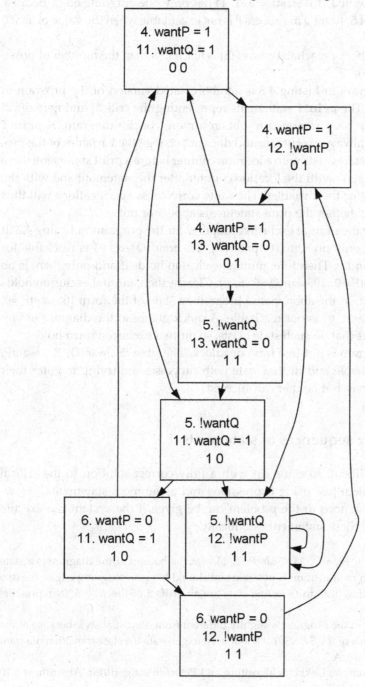

from process P or from process Q. However, the fourth state from the top labeled (5. !wantQ, 13. wantQ=0, 1, 1) has only one outgoing edge, because the statement 5. !wantQ in process P is not executable when the value of wantQ is true (= 1).[4]

The number of reachable states (8) is *much* less than the number of possible states (36).

The program in Listing 4.3 is an abbreviated version of the program in Listing 4.2.[5] The **printf** statements representing the critical and noncritical sections have been removed to obtain a more concise diagram. A **printf** statement is always executable and does not change the variables of the program, so if a state exists with a location counter before a print statement, there also exists a state with the location counter after the statement and with the same values for the variables. The same correctness specifications will thus be provable whether the print statements appear or not.

Consider the mutual exclusion property for the program in Listing 4.2. It holds if and only no state (8. printf(P), 18. printf(Q), x, y) is reachable for arbitrary x and y. Therefore, mutual exclusion holds if and only there is no state (9. wantP=0, 19. wantQ=0, x, y). Clearly, then, mutual exclusion holds if and only if, in the abbreviated program, a state of the form (6. wantP=0, 13. wantQ=0, x, y) is not reachable. A quick glance at the diagram in Figure 4.1 shows that no such state exists, so mutual exclusion must hold.

The program is not free from deadlock. The state (5. !wantQ, 12. !wantP, 1, 1) is reachable and in that state both processes are trying to enter their critical sections, but neither can succeed.

4.4 Atomic sequences of statements

It is quite difficult to come up with a fully correct solution to the critical section problem just using expressions and assignment statements.[6] However, easy solutions to the problem can be given if the system can execute sequences of these statements atomically.

---

[4] The state (5. !wantQ, 11. !wantP, 1, 1) near the bottom of the diagram is a state from which no transition is possible and should have no outgoing edges; the two edges curving back to the same state are an artifact of the way SPIN represents such a state.

[5] The layout of the program is slightly different from our usual style because of the requirements of the SPINSPIDER tool used to generate the state transition diagram (see Appendix A.3.)

[6] See, for example, Dekker's algorithm and Peterson's algorithm, Algorithms 3.10 and 3.13 in *PCDP*.

The program in Listing 4.4 contains a potentially blocking expression and an assignment statement as one atomic sequence of statements (lines 6–9, 18–21). This ensures that once process P has checked that !wantQ is true, it is not possible for process Q to set wantQ to true before P sets wantP to true.

Listing 4.4. Atomic sequences of statements

```
1   bool wantP = false, wantQ = false;
2
3   active proctype P() {
4     do
5     :: printf("Noncritical section P\n");
6        atomic {
7           !wantQ;
8           wantP = true
9        }
10       printf("Critical section P\n");
11       wantP = false
12    od
13  }
14
15  active proctype Q() {
16    do
17    :: printf("Noncritical section Q\n");
18       atomic {
19          !wantP;
20          wantQ = true
21       }
22       printf("Critical section Q\n");
23       wantQ = false
24    od
25  }
```

In Listing 4.4, the potentially blocking statements (the expression !wantQ at line 7 and the expression !wantP at line 19) are at the beginning of the atomic sequences. Therefore, the atomic sequence may be blocked from executing, but once it starts executing, both statements are executed without interference from the other process.

Verify that this program fulfils the correctness requirements of mutual exclusion and of absence of deadlock. However, starvation is possible; the techniques for verifying this property and for finding a counterexample are presented in Chapter 5.

4.4.1 d_step and atomic*

In Section 3.7 we mentioned that there are two constructs in PROMELA for specifying that a sequence of statements must be executed atomically: **d_step** and **atomic**.

The advantage of **d_step** is that it is extremely efficient because the statements of the sequence are executed or verified as a single step in a fully deterministic manner. However, there are three limitations on **d_step**:

- Except for the first statement in the sequence (the guard), statements cannot block.
- It is illegal to jump into the sequence or out of it using **goto** or **break**.
- Nondeterminism is always resolved by choosing the first true alternative in a guarded command. For example, if a equals b in the following code, the value of branch will always equal 1:

```
d_step {
  if
  :: a >= b -> max = a; branch = 1
  :: b >= a -> max = b; branch = 2
  fi
}
```

d_step is usually reserved for fragments of sequential code, while **atomic** is preferred for implementing synchronization primitives.

Consider the program in Listing 4.5, which models an unreliable component for relaying data. Process Source generates values for input and the Process Destination prints the values of output. Process Relay transfers data from the Source to the Destination. The **atomic** sequence (lines 13–20) waits until the variable input has data and then waits until the variable output is empty (modeled by zero); then, it nondeterministically either transfers the value from input to output or it ignores the data. The program works as expected and repeated random simulations print out different subsequences of the input sequence.

If **atomic** is replaced by **d_step**, two problems occur. First, since nondeterminism is resolved deterministically in favor of the first alternative, no data are ever dropped at line 18, and the output sequence is always the same

Listing 4.5. Unreliable relay

```
1   #include "for.h"
2   byte input, output;
3
4   active proctype Source() {
5     for (i, 1, 10)
6       input == 0; /* Wait until empty */
7       input = i
8     rof (i)
9   }
10
11  active proctype Relay() {
12    do
13    :: atomic {
14         input != 0;
15         output == 0;
16         if
17         :: output = input
18         :: skip /* Drop input data */
19         fi
20       }
21       input = 0
22    od
23  }
24
25  active proctype Destination() {
26    do
27    :: output != 0; /* Wait until full */
28       printf("Output = %d\n", output);
29       output = 0
30    od
31  }
```

as the input sequence. Second, it is not legal to block at line 15 which is within the **d_step** sequence; this can be modeled, for example, by using a for-loop with an upper bound less than ten instead of the nonterminating **do**-statement in Destination.

An unreliable relay can also be modeled using channels (Chapter 7):

```
active proctype Relay() {
  byte i;
  do
  :: atomic {
       input ? i;
       if
       :: output ! i
       :: skip
       fi
     }
  od
}
```

Again, changing **atomic** to **d_step** cancels the nondeterministic selection of an alternative and can cause an error at the output statement output ! i if the channel is full or if a rendezvous channel is used and the process Destination is not ready.

4.5 Semaphores

Atomic sequences of statements can be used to model synchronization primitives such as semaphores. The most widely known construct for synchronizing concurrent programs is the *semaphore*. Here is a simple definition of a semaphore using concepts of PROMELA:

A semaphore sem is a variable of type **byte** (nonnegative integers). There are two *atomic* operations defined for a semaphore:
- wait(sem): The operation is executable when the value of sem is positive; executing the operation decrements the value of sem.
- signal(sem): The operation is always executable; executing the operation increments the value of sem.

Listing 4.6 shows a solution to the critical section problem using semaphores. The wait operation is implemented using **atomic** to ensure that the value of sem is decremented only when it is positive (lines 6–9, 18–21). The signal operation needs no special implementation because the assignment statement is atomic (lines 11, 23). Verify that the program fulfils the correctness properties of mutual exclusion and absence of deadlock.

Listing 4.6. The critical section problem with semaphores

```
1   byte sem = 1;
2
3   active proctype P() {
4     do
5     :: printf("Noncritical section P\n");
6        atomic {   /* wait(sem) */
7           sem > 0;
8           sem--
9        }
10       printf("Critical section P\n");
11       sem++        /* signal(sem) */
12    od
13  }
14
15  active proctype Q() {
16    do
17    :: printf("Noncritical section Q\n");
18       atomic {   /* wait(sem) */
19          sem > 0;
20          sem--
21       }
22       printf("Critical section Q\n");
23       sem++        /* signal(sem) */
24    od
25  }
```

Advanced: Fairness of semaphores

The subject of semaphores is more complex than this simple example indicates. The difficulties arise when we try to define the *fairness* of the semaphore operations. Even when a verification is performed with weak fairness enabled (see Section 5.5), a computation for starvation is found because process Q can enter its critical section repeatedly while P does not.

In this computation, the only process that executes is process Q, which repeatedly executes its entire loop from line 16 to 24. The computation is weakly fair because P is enabled infinitely often (after Q executes sem++ at line 23); the nonfair computation simply chooses not to execute the atomic statement from P when it is enabled.

The signal operation is usually defined to unblock one of the processes blocked on the semaphore (if any) as part of its atomic operation. A *strong semaphore* implements the set of blocked processes as a FIFO (first in-first out) queue; this is easy to model in PROMELA using channels (Chapter 7). The signal operation of a *weak semaphore* unblocks an arbitrary element of the set; weak semaphores are harder to model in PROMELA (see Exercise 6.15 of *PCDP*).

4.6 Nondeterminism in models of concurrent systems

Consider, for example, a communications system that must be able to receive and process an *arbitrary* stream of messages of several different types. A natural approach to modeling this requirement is to generate the messages stream by using a *random number* generator. If there are n message types $m_0, m_1, \ldots, m_{n-1}$, each message in the stream is obtained by generating a random number in the range 0 to $n - 1$.

However, this approach is flawed. While a random number generator can be used to obtain a random computation (and this is precisely what SPIN does in random simulation mode), for verification *all* computations must be checked, not just those that happen to be generated randomly.

By design, SPIN does not contain constructs for modeling probability or for specifying that an event must occur with a certain probability. The intended use of model checking is to detect errors that occur under complex scenarios that are unlikely to be discovered during system testing. "In a well-designed system, erroneous behavior should be impossible, not just improbable" [*SMC*, p. 454].[7]

---

[7] See also the discussion on p. 570 of *SMC*.

In SPIN, nondeterminism is used to model arbitrary values of data: whenever a value – such as a message type in a stream – is needed, a nondeterministic choice is made among all values in the range.

4.6.1 Generating values nondeterministically

Suppose that we want to model a client-server system in which the client *nondeterministically* chooses which request to make; we can use an **if**-statement whose guards are always true:[8]

```
active proctype Client() {
  if
  :: true -> request = 1
  :: true -> request = 2
  fi;
  /* Wait for service */
  if
  :: true -> request = 1
  :: true -> request = 2
  fi;
  /* Wait for service */
}
```

The code can be shortened by doing away with the expressions **true** which serve no purpose. Instead, the assignment statements themselves – which are always executable – can be used as guards:[9]

```
active proctype Client() {
  if
  :: request = 1
  :: request = 2
  fi;
  /* Wait for service */
  if
  :: request = 1
  :: request = 2
  fi;
  /* Wait for service */
}
```

---

[8] You may want to study the program in Section 4.7.2 before reading this section.

[9] The arrows are also not needed; they are just syntactic sugar for semicolons that are separators, but since there is only one statement in each alternative there is nothing to separate (Section 1.6).

In a random simulation, SPIN randomly chooses which alternative of an **if**-statement to execute; here, the choice is between both alternatives of the statement since they are both executable. In a verification, SPIN chooses the first alternative and searches for a counterexample; if one is not found, it *backtracks* and continues the search from the state that results from choosing the second alternative.

Of course, it doesn't make sense to model a client that generates only two requests. A **do**-statement can be used to model a client that generates an unending stream of requests in an arbitrary order:

```
active proctype Client() {
  do
  :: request = 1;
     /* Wait for service */
  :: request = 2;
     /* Wait for service */
  od
}
```

In Chapter 7 we will discuss some of the correctness properties that can be checked for client-server systems.

4.6.2 Generating from an arbitrary range*

We have shown how to model nondeterministically generated values from a small range:

```
byte number;
if
:: number = 1
:: number = 2
:: number = 3
:: number = 4
fi
```

As the range of values gets larger, it becomes inconvenient to write alternatives for each value. The following PROMELA code shows how to choose nondeterministically values from an arbitrary range, in this case from 0 to 9:

```
#define LOW 0
#define HIGH 9
   byte number = LOW;
   do
   :: number < HIGH -> number++
   :: break
   od
```

As long as the value of number is less than HIGH, both alternatives are executable and SPIN can choose either one. If it chooses the first one, the value of number is incremented; if it chooses the second, the loop is left and the current value of number is used in the subsequent code. It follows that the final value of number can be any value within the range.

To check that 9 is, in fact, a possible value of number, add the assertion

```
   assert (number != HIGH)
```

after the **do**-statement and run a verification. You will get a counterexample and this computation can be examined by running a guided simulation.

Do not put any faith in the uniformity of the probability distribution of the "random numbers" generated using this technique. Assuming that SPIN chooses uniformly between alternatives in the **do**-statement, the first value 0 has a probability of $1/2$ while the last value 9 has a probability of 2^{-10}. Nondeterminism is used to generate arbitrary computations for verification, not random numbers for a faithful simulation.

4.7 Termination of processes

4.7.1 Deadlock

Unfortunately, the program in Listing 4.2 is not a correct solution of the critical section problem. The processes of the program consist of loops with no **goto** or **break** statements, so the program should never terminate.[10] If you run several random simulations of the program, you will likely encounter a computation in which execution terminates with the output timeout. This means that *no* statements are executable, a condition called *deadlock*.[11]

It is quite easy to construct the computation that leads to deadlock. Simply execute statements in perfect interleaving (one statement alternately from each process); both wantP and wantQ are set to true (lines 6, 16) and

---

[10] When running a simulation in SPIN, you normally limit of the number of statements that can be executed by using the argument -uN (see Section 1.2).

[11] timeout is discussed further in Section 8.1.1.

then both processes are blocked waiting for the other one to set its variable to false (lines 7, 17).

An attempt at verification will discover an error called an *invalid end state*:

```
pan: invalid end state (at depth 8)
```

By default, a process that does terminate must do so after executing its last instruction, otherwise it is said to be in an invalid end state. This error is checked for regardless of any other correctness specifications. This default behavior can be overridden as described in the next subsection.

4.7.2 End states*

Consider the program in Listing 4.7. There are two server processes supplying different services and one client process that requests service 1 and then service 2. The client process indicates which service it needs by setting the variable request to the number of the service; it then blocks waiting for the expression request == 0 to become true. The guard of the alternative in one of the server processes is now true, so it can provide the service (represented by a **printf** statement). Then, the server resets request to zero to indicate that the service is complete; this unblocks the client.

This PROMELA program is a reasonable model of a very simple *client-server system*.[12] However, if you simulate or verify it in SPIN, you will receive an error message that there is an invalid end state. The reason is that while the client executes a finite number of statements and then terminates, the servers are always blocked at the guard of the **do**-statement waiting for it to become executable. Now, this is acceptable behavior because servers should wait indefinitely and be ready to supply a service whenever it is needed. Since the server cannot know how many requests it will receive, it is unreasonable to require termination of a process modeling a server.

You can indicate that a control point within a process is to be considered a valid end point even though it is not the last statement of the process by prefixing it with a label that begins with end:

```
active proctype Server1() {
endserver:
  do
  :: request == 1 -> . . .
  od
}
```

---

[12] Client-server systems are presented more systematically in Chapter 7.

Listing 4.7. A client-server program with end states

```
1  byte request = 0;
2
3  active proctype Server1() {
4    do
5    :: request == 1 ->
6         printf("Service 1\n");
7         request = 0
8    od
9  }
10
11 active proctype Server2() {
12   do
13   :: request == 2 ->
14        printf("Service 2\n");
15        request = 0
16   od
17 }
18
19 active proctype Client() {
20   request = 1;
21   request == 0;
22   request = 2;
23   request == 0
24 }
```

Add end labels to both server processes in the program in Listing 4.7 and show that a verification no longer reports an invalid end state.

An alternate way of ignoring end states is to ask SPIN to refrain from reporting invalid end states during a verification:

jSpin

Select Options / Pan and add the argument -E. Be sure to remove the argument when it is no longer needed.

Command line

Add the argument -E to the pan command for running the verifier.

The program in Listing 4.2 *does* fulfil the requirement of mutual exclusion; this can be shown using the technique described in Listing 3.8: counting the number of processes in their critical sections and asserting that the value of the variable is less than or equal to 1. If you run a verification, be sure to turn off checking of invalid end states as described above.

4.7.3 The order of process termination*

A process *terminates* when it has reached the end of its code, but it is considered to be an active process until it *dies*. SPIN manages process allocation in the LIFO (last in-first out) order of a stack, so a process can die only if it is the most recent process that was created. Usually, the distinction between process termination and death is not an issue, but it can sometimes explain why a program does not end as expected.

Process termination and death are demonstrated by the program in Listing 4.8. The two servers each perform one service and then terminate, incrementing the variable finished that counts the number of processes that have terminated. Since processes created by **active proctype** are instantiated in the order written, the two server processes do not die until the client process finds finished == 2 and terminates.

The output is just as we expect it to be:

```
11:    proc  2 (Client) terminates
11:    proc  1 (Server2) terminates
11:    proc  0 (Server1) terminates
```

Suppose now that we change line 21 to finished == 3 so that the client process does not terminate. By the LIFO rule, the server processes will not terminate, and the simulation goes into a state called timeout in which no process is at an executable statement:

```
timeout
#processes: 3
2 Client          2          0
1 Server          2          0
0 Server          2          0
```

All three processes are still active, though none are executable.

Listing 4.8. Client-server termination

```
1   byte request = 0;
2   byte finished = 0;
3
4   active proctype Server1() {
5     request == 1;
6     request = 0;
7     finished++
8   }
9
10  active proctype Server2() {
11    request == 2;
12    request = 0;
13    finished++
14  }
15
16  active proctype Client() {
17    request = 1;
18    request == 0;
19    request = 2;
20    request == 0;
21    finished == 2;
22  }
```

Next, move the process Client so that it appears *before* the server processes in the source code. Now, the server processes are created after the client process so they can terminate without waiting for the client process, which is blocked, hopelessly waiting for finished to receive the value 3:

```
timeout
#processes: 1
0 Client                    2            0
```

5

Verification with Temporal Logic

In Sections 3.8 and 3.9 we showed how to use assertions to specify and verify correctness properties of concurrent programs written in PROMELA. However, assertions are not sufficient to specify and verify most correctness properties of models. This chapter presents *linear temporal logic (LTL)*, which is the formal logic used for verification in SPIN.[1] We start with an informal description of correctness properties more advanced than assertions. This is followed by an introduction to the syntax and semantics of LTL, an explanation of how to specify correctness properties in LTL, and a description of the techniques for using SPIN to verify that an LTL formula holds for a model. Section 5.9 gives an overview of more advanced ways of expressing properties in temporal logic. For a definitive treatment of LTL, see [16, 17].

5.1 Beyond assertions

Assertions are limited in the properties that they can specify because they are attached to specific control points in the processes. For example, in order to verify that mutual exclusion holds for a solution to the critical section problem, we inserted the following code at the control points representing the critical section in *each* process:

```
critical++;
assert (critical <= 1);
critical--;
```

---

[1] There are many forms of temporal logic; one, *computational tree logic (CTL)*, is also used extensively in verification [8]. Since SPIN limits itself to supporting LTL, the use of the term "temporal logic" in this book refers to LTL.

Usually, however, it is necessary or at least more convenient to express a correctness property as a global property of the system that is not associated with specific control points. Here are several examples of such properties:

- **Mutual exclusion**
  Mutual exclusion can be expressed as a global invariant:
  In every state of every computation, `critical <= 1`.

- **Absence of deadlock (invalid end states)**
  A PROMELA program is said to deadlock if it enters an invalid end state (Sections 4.7.1–4.7.2); this can be expressed as a global invariant:
  In every state of every computation, if no statements are executable, the location counter of each process must be at the end of the process or at a statement labeled end.
  This correctness property is checked automatically by SPIN.

- **Array index bounds**
  Let a be an array, let LEN be the length of the array, and let i be a variable used to index the array. An important global invariant is:
  In every state of every computation, $0 <= i <= LEN-1$.
  This formula could be added as an assertion after every statement that assigns a new value to i, but it is easier to specify that it holds in every state. This avoids errors caused if you forget to attach an assertion to one of the relevant statements.

- **Quantity invariant**
  In distributed algorithms called *token-passing algorithms*, mutual exclusion is achieved by passing a *token* – an explicit representation of the permission to enter the critical section – among the processes (see Sections 10.6 and 10.7 of *PCDP*). A global invariant that must hold in such algorithms is:
  In every state of every computation, there is at most one token in existence.

Furthermore, there are some correctness properties that simply cannot be expressed using assertions, because the properties cannot be checked by evaluating an expression in a *single state* of a computation. For example, in the critical section problem the following two properties are expressed as relations between two states of the computation: a state *s* in which processes are trying to enter their critical sections, and a state *t* in which a process does enter it. *t* may occur thousands of states later in the computation than *s*:

- **Absence of deadlock**[2]

  In every state of every computation, if some processes are trying to enter their critical sections, eventually some process *does so.*

- **Absence of starvation**

  In every state of every computation, if a process tries to enter its critical section, eventually that process *does so.*

A correctness specification like the ones given in this section is expressed in SPIN by a finite automaton called a *never claim* that is is executed together with the finite automaton that represents the PROMELA program. Specifying a correctness property directly as a never claim is difficult; instead, a formula written in linear temporal logic is translated by SPIN into a never claim, which is then used for verification. A brief introduction to never claims is given in Section 10.3, but for most purposes you need not concern yourself with never claims and can work entirely with LTL formulas.

The next section presents LTL as a formal logic. This is followed by sections describing how to express correctness properties of models in LTL and how to carry out verifications in SPIN.

5.2 Introduction to linear temporal logic

5.2.1 The syntax of LTL

LTL is based upon the propositional calculus; formulas of the propositional calculus are composed from atomic propositions (denoted by letters $p, q, \ldots$) and the operators:

Operator	Math	SPIN
not	$\neg$	!
and	$\wedge$	&&
or	$\vee$	||
implies	$\rightarrow$	->
equivalent	$\leftrightarrow$	<->

We have given both the usual mathematical symbols and the syntax used for writing formulas in SPIN; here is a formula written in both notations:

$$(p \wedge \neg q) \rightarrow (p \vee \neg q), \qquad (p \ \&\& \ !q) \ -> \ (p \ || \ !q).$$

---

[2] The deadlock (invalid end states) described previously states that the computation cannot continue; this specification of deadlock states that the computation can continue, but processes cannot enter their critical sections.

A formula of LTL is built from atomic propositions and from operators that include the operators of the propositional calculus as well as temporal operators. The atomic propositions of LTL are described in the next subsection. The temporal operators are:

Operator	Math	SPIN
always	$\square$	[]
eventually	$\diamond$	<>
until	$\mathcal{U}$	U

The $\square$ and $\diamond$ operators are unary and the $\mathcal{U}$ operator is binary. Temporal and propositional operators combine freely, so the following formula (given in both mathematical and PROMELA notation) is syntactically correct:

$$\square((p \wedge q) \rightarrow r\,\mathcal{U}(p \vee r)), \qquad []((p \&\& q) \;\text{->}\; r \; U \; (p \;||\; r)).$$

Read this as:

Always, (p and q) implies that r holds until (p or r) holds.

5.2.2 The semantics of LTL

The semantics, the meaning, of a syntactically correct formula is defined by giving it an *interpretation*: an assignment of truth values, T (true) or F (false), to its atomic propositions and the extension of the assignment to an interpretation of the entire formula according to the rules for the operators. For the propositional calculus these are given by the familiar *truth tables*, where A and B are any formulas:

A	B	$\neg A$	$A \wedge B$	$A \vee B$	$A \rightarrow B$	$A \leftrightarrow B$
T	T	F	T	T	T	T
T	F	F	F	T	F	F
F	T	T	F	T	T	F
F	F	T	F	F	T	T

For temporal logic, the semantics of a formula is given in terms of computations and the states of a computation. The atomic propositions of temporal logic are boolean expressions that can be evaluated in a single state *independently* of a computation. For example, let *critical* be the value of the variable critical in a program for the critical section problem; the expression *critical* ≤ 1 is an atomic proposition because it can be assigned a truth value in a state s just by checking the value of the variable critical in s. Similarly, if *csp* is a boolean expression that is true if and only if the location counter

Fig. 5.1. State diagram for the third attempt

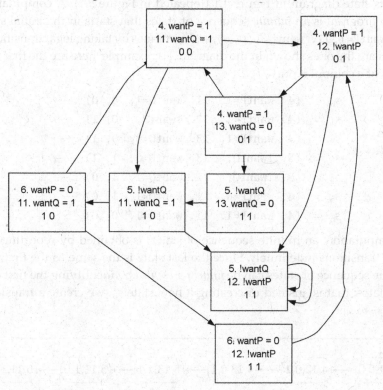

of process P is at the control point corresponding to the critical section of the process, then *csp* is an atomic proposition because it can be evaluated in any single state.

Atomic propositions can be combined using the operators of the propositional calculus; such formulas can also be evaluated just by checking values in a single state. For example, if *csq* is similar to *csp* but for process Q, the expression $\neg(csp \wedge csq)$ specifies that mutual exclusion holds *in the state in which it is evaluated.*

Consider again the program for the critical section problem in Listing 4.3 and its state diagram in Figure 4.1 (repeated in Figure 5.1). A computation of the program is an *infinite* sequence of states that starts in the initial state (4. wantP=1, 11. wantQ=1, 0, 0), and continues by taking legal transitions, which are the ones shown in the diagram. For example, here are the first few states of a computation:

$$
\begin{aligned}
s_0 &= \text{(4. wantP=1, 11. wantQ=1, 0, 0)} \longrightarrow \\
s_1 &= \text{(4. wantP=1, 12. !wantP, 0, 1)} \longrightarrow \\
s_2 &= \text{(4. wantP=1, 13. wantQ=0, 0, 1)} \longrightarrow \\
s_3 &= \text{(5. !wantQ, 13. wantQ=0, 1, 1)} \longrightarrow \\
s_4 &= \text{(5. !wantQ, 11. wantQ=1, 1, 0)} \longrightarrow \\
s_5 &= \text{(6. wantP=0, 11. wantQ=1, 1, 0)} \longrightarrow \\
s_6 &= \text{(4. wantP=1, 11. wantQ=1, 0, 0)}
\end{aligned}
$$

A computation, an infinite sequence of states, is obtained by repeating the same transitions indefinitely. Since the last state is the same as the first, the infinite sequence of states can be *finitely presented* by identifying the first and last states; that is, instead of creating a new state s_6, we create a transition from s_5 to s_0:[3]

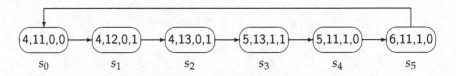

Process P is in its critical section if its location counter is at line 6 and process Q is in its critical section if its location counter is at line 13. Let *csp* and *csq* be atomic propositions representing these properties. Clearly, *for the computation shown above*, the formula $\neg(csp \wedge csq)$ that expresses the correctness property of mutual exclusion is true in *all* its states.

We have shown that this formula is true for one specific computation, but since there are no states in which process P is at line 6 and process Q is at line 13, we can generalize and claim that the following statement is true:

The formula $\neg(csp \wedge csq)$ is true in every state of every computation.

Let us now show how to express this property in LTL and how to verify that the property holds for the program in Listing 4.3.

---

[3] In this diagram, the values of the location counters are indicated by line numbers without the source code.

5.3 Safety properties

5.3.1 Expressing safety properties in LTL

Let A be an LTL formula and let $\tau = (s_0, s_1, s_2, \ldots)$ be a computation. Then $\Box A$, read *always A*, is true in state s_i if and only if A is true *for all* s_j in τ such that $j \geq i$.

The operator is reflexive so if $\Box A$ is true in a state s, then A must also be true in s. The formula $\Box A$ is called a *safety property* because it specifies that the computation is safe in that nothing "bad" ever happens, or equivalently, that the only things that happen are "good."

We can draw a diagram of a computation, labeling each state s_i with A if A is true in s_i and with $\neg A$ if A is false in s_i. If the following diagram is extended indefinitely with all states labeled A, then $\Box A$ is true in s_0:

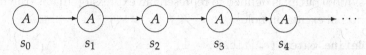

The correctness property of mutual exclusion can be expressed by the LTL formula $\Box \neg (csp \wedge csq)$. This is a safety property because it is true if something "bad" – $csp \wedge csq$, meaning the two processes in their critical section – never happens. Equivalently, the only states the computation enters are "good" ones in which $\neg (csp \wedge csq)$ is true.

Important: In linear temporal logic, each formula implicitly refers to *all* computations of a model. Therefore, when a correctness property for a model is specified by an LTL formula, it means that the property holds if the formula is true in *all* computations of the model. If SPIN finds even a single counterexample – a computation in which the formula is false – the correctness property does not hold for the model.

5.3.2 Expressing safety properties in PROMELA

For the program in Listing 4.3 we verified that mutual exclusion holds by writing **assert** statements in each critical section. It is also possible to express this property in LTL. As before, we declare a variable `critical`, incrementing it at the beginning of each critical section and decrementing it at the end:

```
active proctype P() {
  do
  :: wantP = true;
     !wantQ;
     critical++;
     critical--;
     wantP = false;
  od
}
```

```
/* Similarly for process Q */
```

Since the critical section in the abbreviated program is not explicitly written, the statement critical-- immediately follows the statement critical++, and the critical section is the control point between them.

The symbol mutex is defined to represent an expression that is true if and only if mutual exclusion holds:

```
#define mutex (critical <= 1)
```

Mutual exclusion can now be specified in PROMELA by the LTL formula:

```
[]mutex
```

Alternatively, we could define two variables csp and csq of boolean type, and set these variables to indicate when a process is in its critical section:

```
active proctype P() {
  do
  :: wantP = true;
     !wantQ;
     csp = true;
     csp = false;
     wantP = false;
  od
}
```

```
/* Similarly, for process Q */
```

The LTL formula expressing mutual exclusion is now

```
[]!(csp && csq)
```

A third way of expressing this property that does not use ghost variables is described in Section 5.7.

Fig. 5.2. Verifying a safety property in jSPIN

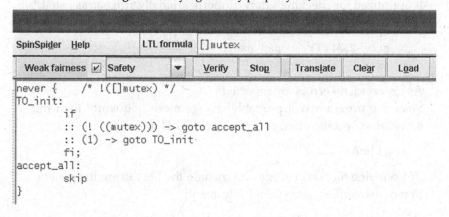

```
SpinSpider  Help          LTL formula  []mutex

 Weak fairness ☑ Safety        ▼    Verify   Stop   Translate   Clear   Load
never {      /* !([]mutex) */
T0_init:
       if
       :: (! ((mutex))) -> goto accept_all
       :: (1) -> goto T0_init
       fi;
accept_all:
       skip
}
```

5.3.3 Verifying safety properties in SPIN

This section shows how to verify safety properties in SPIN.

jSpin

The upper right corner of the JSPIN display contains the interface that is used to enter LTL formulas and to perform verifications (Figure 5.2). Write the LTL formula in the text field provided and select Translate. The formula is saved in a file with the same name as the PROMELA source file and with extension prp; then SPIN is called to translate the formula into a never claim, which is displayed in the right pane (though you may ignore it) and saved in a file with extension ltl.

Ensure that Safety is selected for the verification mode and select Verify. SPIN will perform the verification and display the result in the right pane. In this case, no errors are found so we have proved that mutual exclusion holds for this program.

There are three other buttons related to LTL formulas in the JSPIN interface. Clear clears the field for the LTL formula and ensures that subsequent verification runs will not use the contents of the field. Load brings up a file chooser to load an LTL formula from a prp file. Stop terminates a verification if it is taking too much time.

Command line

To verify a safety property, first add the *negation* of the LTL formula with the -f argument to the SPIN command that generates the verifier. Then, compile the verifier with the –DSAFETY argument so that it is optimized for checking safety properties. Finally, run pan as usual:[4]

```
spin -a -f "![]mutex" third-safety.pml
gcc -DSAFETY -o pan pan.c
pan
```

As expected, no errors are reported.

Since the program will probably change more frequently than the correctness specification, you can save the LTL formula

```
![]mutex
```

in a one-line file safety.prp and include the file during the generation of the verifier using the –F argument:

```
spin -a -F safety.prp third-safety.pml
```

Alternatively, the translation of the LTL formula to a never claim can be saved in a file and this file included in the generation of the verifier using the –N argument:

```
spin -a -f "![]mutex"  > safety.ltl
spin -a -N safety.ltl third-safety.pml
```

If the verification seems to be taking too much time, you can terminate it as you would terminate any program (ctrl-C).

Warning

Atomic propositions in an LTL formula must be identifiers starting with a lower-case letter.

Furthermore, they must be boolean variables or defined as symbols for boolean-valued expressions.

Warning

Section 10.3 explains why the correctness specification must be negated. This is done automatically in JSPIN, but if you run SPIN from the command line, be sure to do it yourself.

---

[4] You may need to use single quotes instead of double quotes.

Warning

SPIN runs in a separate process that is forked from the process that runs JSPIN, so it is possible to terminate JSPIN without terminating SPIN. In that case, your computer may start to run slowly if SPIN is executing a long verification or a simulation of an infinite loop, and you will have to terminate SPIN manually.

In Windows this is done by pressing `ctrl-alt-del` to bring up the `Task Manager`, then selecting `Task List` and `Processes` and selecting `End Process` for each occurrence of `spin.exe` or `pan.exe`.

5.4 Liveness properties

Let A be a formula of LTL and let $\tau = (s_0, s_1, s_2, \ldots)$ be a computation. Then $\Diamond A$, read *eventually A*, is true in state s_i if and only if A is true *for some s_j in τ such that $j \geq i$.*

The operator is reflexive, so if A is true in a state s, then so is $\Diamond A$. The formula $\Diamond A$ is called a *liveness property* because it specifies that something "good" eventually happens in the computation.

If *csp* is the atomic proposition that is true in a state if process P is in its critical section, then $\Diamond csp$ holds if and only if process P eventually enters its critical section.[5]

It is essential that correctness specifications contain liveness properties because a safety property is vacuously satisfied by an empty program that does nothing! For example, a solution to the critical section problem in which neither process tries to enter its critical section trivially fulfils the correctness properties of mutual exclusion and absence of deadlock:

```
start:
  do
  :: printf("Noncritical section\n");
     goto start;
     wantP = true; /* Try to enter the critical section */
     printf("Critical section\n")
  od
```

---

[5] A better way of specifying absence of starvation is presented in Section 5.9.2.

5.4.1 Expressing liveness properties in SPIN

Listing 5.1 shows a program for the critical section problem.[6] We leave it to the reader to verify that both mutual exclusion and absence of deadlock hold. Unfortunately, this program is not fully correct because starvation may occur, that is, there is a computation in which process P never enters its critical section:

Listing 5.1. Critical section with starvation

```
1   bool wantP = false, wantQ = false;
2
3   active proctype P() {
4     do
5     :: wantP = true;
6        do
7        :: wantQ ->
8              wantP = false;
9              wantP = true
10       :: else -> break
11       od;
12       wantP = false
13     od
14  }
15
16  active proctype Q() {
17    do
18    :: wantQ = true;
19       do
20       :: wantP ->
21             wantQ = false;
22             wantQ = true
23       :: else -> break
24       od;
25       wantQ = false
26    od
27  }
```

---

[6] This is the *fourth attempt* described in Section 3.8 of *PCDP*.

$$s_0 = (5.\ \text{wantP=1},\quad 18.\ \text{wantQ=1},\quad 0,\ 0) \longrightarrow$$
$$s_1 = (5.\ \text{wantP=1},\quad 20.\ \text{wantP},\quad 0,\ 1) \longrightarrow$$
$$s_2 = (5.\ \text{wantP=1},\quad 25.\ \text{wantQ=0},\quad 0,\ 1) \longrightarrow$$
$$s_3 = (7.\ \text{wantQ},\quad 25.\ \text{wantQ=0},\quad 1,\ 1) \longrightarrow$$
$$s_4 = (8.\ \text{wantP=0},\quad 25.\ \text{wantQ=0},\quad 1,\ 1) \longrightarrow$$
$$s_5 = (9.\ \text{wantP=1},\quad 25.\ \text{wantQ=0},\quad 0,\ 1) \longrightarrow$$
$$s_6 = (9.\ \text{wantP=1},\quad 18.\ \text{wantQ=1},\quad 0,\ 0) \longrightarrow$$
$$s_7 = (9.\ \text{wantP=1},\quad 20.\ \text{wantP},\quad 0,\ 1) \longrightarrow$$
$$s_8 = (9.\ \text{wantP=1},\quad 25.\ \text{wantQ=0},\quad 0,\ 1) \longrightarrow$$
$$s_9 = (7.\ \text{wantQ},\quad 25.\ \text{wantQ=0},\quad 1,\ 1)$$

Since state s_9 is the same as state s_3, they can be identified and the sequence of states extended to an infinite computation:

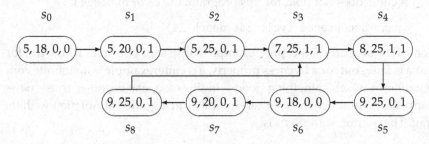

The critical section of process P (line 12) does not appear in any state of this computation, demonstrating that absence of starvation does not hold for this program.

5.4.2 Verifying liveness properties in SPIN

Add the statements

```
csp = true;
csp = false;
```

between lines 11 and 12 of the program in Listing 5.1; then the LTL formula <>csp expresses absence of starvation for process P. The verification of the temporal formula is carried out in a manner similar to that of the safety property, except that it must be performed in a mode called searching for *acceptance cycles* (Section 10.3.2). *Weak fairness*, explained in Section 5.5, must also be specified when this program is verified.

jSpin

Select Acceptance instead of Safety from the pulldown menu, and ensure that the box labeled Weak fairness is checked. Select Verify.

Command line

Run the verifier with the –a (*a*cceptance) argument and the –f (weak *f*airness) argument:[7]

```
spin -a -f "!<>csp" fourth-liveness.pml
gcc -o pan pan.c
pan -a -f
```

Liveness does not hold for this program; the error message is

```
pan: acceptance cycle (at depth 14)
```

For safety properties, a counterexample consists of one state where the formula is false, but for a liveness property, a counterexample is an infinite computation in which something good – in this case, csp becomes true – never happens. To produce the counterexample, run a guided simulation with the trail. The output from JSPIN is:

Process	Statement	wantQ	wantP
1 Q	wantQ = 1		
1 Q	wantQ = 0	1	
0 P	wantP = 1	0	
1 Q	wantQ = 1	1	0
1 Q	wantP	1	1
0 P	wantQ	1	1
<<<<<START OF CYCLE>>>>>			
1 Q	wantQ = 0	1	1
1 Q	wantQ = 1	1	0
1 Q	wantP	1	1
0 P	wantP = 0	1	1
1 Q	wantQ = 0	0	1
1 Q	wantQ = 1	0	0
0 P	wantP = 1	0	1
0 P	wantQ	1	1
1 Q	wantQ = 0	1	1
0 P	wantP = 0	1	0

---

[7] Ensure that the –DSAFETY argument is not used in the compilation.

1 Q	wantQ = 1	0	0
1 Q	wantQ = 0	0	1
0 P	wantP = 1	0	0
1 Q	wantQ = 1	1	0
1 Q	wantP	1	1
0 P	wantQ	1	1

```
spin: trail ends after 50 steps
```

The line START OF CYCLE indicates that the subsequent states form a cycle that can be repeated indefinitely. Since a variable appears in the SPIN output only when it is assigned to, the absence of a value for csp means that the variable has never been assigned to and hence that starvation occurs in this computation.

Advanced: Finding the shortest counterexamples

SPIN did not find the *shortest* counterexample. That is because SPIN performs a depth-first search of the state diagram and stops with the first counterexample it finds. The -i and -I arguments to pan can be used to perform an iterated search for shorter counterexamples; see pages 24–25 of *SMC* for details.

5.5 Fairness

Consider again the program for the critical section problem in Listing 5.1. Is the following computation a counterexample for the property of absence of starvation?

$$s_0 = (5.\ \text{wantP=1},\ 18.\ \text{wantQ=1},\ 0,\ 0) \longrightarrow$$
$$s_1 = (5.\ \text{wantP=1},\ 20.\ \text{wantP},\quad 0,\ 1) \longrightarrow$$
$$s_2 = (5.\ \text{wantP=1},\ 25.\ \text{wantQ=0},\ 0,\ 1) \longrightarrow$$
$$s_3 = (5.\ \text{wantP=1},\ 18.\ \text{wantQ=1},\ 0,\ 0)$$

State s_3 is identical to s_0, so an infinite computation can be composed from just the three states s_0, s_1, s_2. In this computation, process Q enters its critical section repeatedly, while process P never executes any of its statements. The computation *is* a counterexample to a claim that <>csp is true, but it is unsatisfactory because it doesn't give process P a "fair" chance to try to enter its critical section. This concept can be formalized by the following definition:[8]

A computation is *weakly fair* if and only if the following condition holds: if a statement is *always* executable, then it is *eventually* executed as part of the computation.

---

[8] There is also a concept called *strong fairness*; see Section 2.7 of *PCDP*.

The computation described above is not weakly fair: Although like all assignment statements, 5. wantP = **true** is always executable, it is never executed in the computation. As we have shown, absence of starvation does not, in fact, hold for the program in Listing 5.1, but it seems reasonable to require that only fair computations be considered as counterexamples.

jSpin

Ensure that the box labeled Weak fairness is checked before selecting Verify. (This is the default.)

Command line

Add the argument -f (in addition to the argument -a) when executing the verifier pan.

Warning

Restricting verification to computations that are weakly fair requires a lot of memory. By default, SPIN limits the number of processes to two in a verification with fairness; if there are more processes, you need to compile the verifier with a higher value for the parameter -DNFAIR=n.

We conclude this section with an example of a program whose properties depend critically on fairness (Listing 5.2). The assignment in process Q is always enabled, so in a weakly fair computation it will eventually be executed, causing the loop in process P to terminate. If weak fairness is *not* specified, there is a nonterminating computation in which the **do**-statement is executed indefinitely. Thus the correctness property "the program always terminates" holds if and only if computations are required to be weakly fair.

5.6 Duality

The operators $\Box$ and $\Diamond$ are *dual* in a manner similar to the duality expressed by deMorgan's laws:

$$\neg (p \wedge q) \equiv (\neg p \vee \neg q), \quad \neg (p \vee q) \equiv (\neg p \wedge \neg q).$$

Passing a negation through a unary temporal operator changes the operator to the other one:

$$\neg \Box p \equiv \Diamond \neg p, \quad \neg \Diamond p \equiv \Box \neg p.$$

Listing 5.2. Termination under weak fairness

```
1   int n = 0;
2   bool flag = false;
3
4   active proctype P() {
5     do
6     :: flag -> break
7     :: else -> n = 1 - n
8     od
9   }
10
11  active proctype Q() {
12    flag = true
13  }
```

Since double negations cancel out, duality can be used to simplify formulas with temporal operators. Let *good* and *bad* be atomic propositions such that *good* is equivalent to ¬*bad*. Then we have the following equivalences:

$$\neg\, \Box good \;\equiv\; \Diamond\neg\, good \;\equiv\; \Diamond\neg\neg\, bad \;\equiv\; \Diamond\, bad,$$
$$\neg\, \Diamond good \;\equiv\; \Box\neg\, good \;\equiv\; \Box\neg\neg\, bad \;\equiv\; \Box\, bad.$$

These make sense when read out loud: if it is false that something good is always true, then eventually something bad must happen; if it is false that something good eventually happens, then something bad is always true.

It is important to get used to reasoning with the duality of the temporal operators because negations of correctness specifications are at the foundation of model checking (Section 10.3).

5.7 Verifying correctness without ghost variables*

We have used ghost variables like critical and csp as proxies for control points in a PROMELA program. While this causes no problems in the small programs shown in the book, when modeling large systems you will want to keep the number of variables as small as possible. Ghost variables also unnecessarily complicate graphical representations of the state transition diagrams that are generated by the SPINSPIDER tool (Appendix A.3).

PROMELA supports *remote references* that can be used to refer to control points in correctness specifications, either directly within never claims or in

LTL formulas. For example, in a program for the critical section problem, we can replace the ghost variables by defining labels cs at the control points corresponding to the critical sections of the two processes and then defining a symbol that expresses mutual exclusion using remote references:

```
#define mutex !(P@cs && Q@cs)

active proctype P() {
  do
  :: wantP = true;
     !wantQ;
  cs: wantP = false;
  od
}


/* Similarly for process Q */
```

The expression P@cs returns a nonzero value if and only if the location counter of process P is at the control point labeled by cs. Mutual exclusion holds only if both P@cs and Q@cs cannot be true at the same time, expressed as []mutex. A verification run shows that this formula does indeed hold.

It is also possible to refer to the value of a local variable of a process using the syntax process:variable.

> ### Warning
>
> A remote reference is not a *symbol* so it cannot appear directly within an LTL formula. It can appear in a boolean expression for which a symbol is defined as shown above.

5.8 Modeling a noncritical section*

One of the correctness properties of the critical section problem is that a process be able to enter its critical section infinitely often even if another process fails in its *noncritical* section. This can be modeled in PROMELA by including a nondeterministic **if**-statement in a process that is allowed to fail.

The program in Listing 5.3 is a solution to the critical section problem that achieves mutual exclusion.[9] This can be checked by verifying the safety property shown in Section 5.7: define the symbol mutex as !(P@cs && Q@cs) and verfiy []mutex.

---

[9] This is the *first attempt* described in Chapter 3 of *PCDP*.

Lines 5–8 model the noncritical section: P can nondeterministically choose to do nothing (line 6) or to fail by blocking until **false** becomes true, which, of course, will never occur (line 7).

The program in Listing 5.3 is not a correct solution to the critical section problem, because if process P fails in its noncritical section (by blocking at line 7), process Q will eventually become blocked indefinitely waiting for turn == 2 to become true (line 16).

Listing 5.3. Modeling failure in the noncritical section

```
1   byte  turn = 1;
2
3   active proctype P() {
4      do
5      :: if
6         :: true
7         :: true -> false
8         fi;
9         turn == 1;
10   cs:  turn = 2
11      od
12   }
13
14   active proctype Q() {
15      do
16      :: turn == 2;
17   cs:  turn = 1
18      od
19   }
```

Now add an **if**-statement like the one in lines 5–8 to one of the processes of a correct solution to the critical section problem: Dekker's algorithm (Algorithm 3.10 of *PCDP*) or Peterson's algorithm (Listing 5.4 at the end of this chapter). Define the symbol live as Q@cs and verify the absence of starvation: []<>live. Process P fails only when wantP is false, so process Q can continue entering its critical section infinitely often because the expression at line 17 always evaluates to true regardless of the value of the variable last.

5.9 Advanced temporal specifications*

The temporal operators $\Box$ and $\Diamond$ can be applied to any formula of LTL, so that $\Box\Diamond\Diamond A$ and $\Diamond\Box\Diamond(A \wedge \Box B)$ are syntactically correct. It is beyond the scope of this book to present the deductive theory of LTL: axioms, rules of inferences, and theorems relating to properties of formulas such as associativity and commutivity (see *MLCS*, Chapter 12). We just mention two results:

- A formula with sequences of consecutive occurences of the operators $\Box$ or $\Diamond$ is equivalent to one in which the sequences are collapsed to a single occurrence of the operator. For example, $\Box\Box\Diamond\Diamond A$ is equivalent to $\Box\Diamond A$.
- A formula with any sequence of alternate occurences of the operators $\Box$ and $\Diamond$ is equivalent to one in which the sequence is collapsed into one of the two-operator sequences $\Box\Diamond$ or $\Diamond\Box$. For example, $\Diamond\Box\Diamond A$ is equivalent to $\Box\Diamond A$.

Thus, any sequence of unary temporal operators can be collapsed into a sequence of one or two operators.

The next two subsections describe the use of two-operator sequences in formulas expressing commonly used correctness specifications. This is followed by two subsections on the binary temporal operator $\mathcal{U}$ and a final subsection on the *next* operator, which is rarely used in SPIN.

Temporal logic formulas with more than two or three operators are difficult understand. To help write correctness specifications in temporal logic a set of *patterns* has been developed at Kansas State University. The patterns are classified by properties such as *precedence* and *existence*, as well as by scope such as *before* and *between*. Formulas are given not just for the linear temporal logic used in SPIN but also for other logics used in verification. The address of the website of this project is given in Appendix B.

5.9.1 Latching

The formula $\Diamond\Box A$ expresses a *latching* property: A may not be true initially in a computation, but eventually it becomes true and remains true:

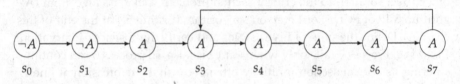

The formula $\Diamond\Box A$ is true in s_0: Although A is not true in s_0 or s_1, it becomes true in s_2 and remains true in all subsequent states of the computation.

Latching is important because it is unusual for a property to be true initially and always; rather, some statements must be executed to make the property true, although once it becomes true, the property remains true. Latching can also express properties that relate to exceptional situations. For example, suppose that a multiprocessor system is designed so that if a processor fails it automatically sets its variables to zero. Then for the program in Listing 5.1, we could claim $\Diamond fails_Q \to \Diamond\Box \neg wantQ$, that is, if ever the processor executing process Q fails, the value of wantQ is latched to false.[10] From this we can deduce that process P will not be starved even if Q fails because eventually the guard wantQ in line 7 will always be false and the **else**-alternative in line 10 can be taken.

5.9.2 Infinitely often

The formula $\Box\Diamond A$ expresses the property that A is true *infinitely often*: A need not always be true, but at *any* state in the computation s, A will be true in s or in some state that comes after s:

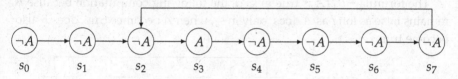

It is easy to see that A is true in the states $s_3, s_9, s_{15}, \ldots$, so at any state s_i, A is true in one of the states $s_i, s_{i+1}, s_{i+2}, s_{i+3}, s_{i+4}, s_{i+5}$.

For solutions to the critical section problem, liveness means not just that a process can enter its critical section, but that it can enter its critical section repeatedly. This can be modeled in PROMELA as follows. First, after setting a variable that indicates that P is in its critical section, we immediately reset it to indicate that P has left its critical section:

```
active proctype P() {
  do
  :: /* Try to enter critical section */
    csp = true;
    csp = false;
    /* Leave critical section */
  od
}
```

---

[10] wantQ can be considered to "belong" to process Q because it is only assigned to in Q, while process P only reads its value.

Then – if the algorithm is free from starvation – we can verify the program for the temporal formula []<>csp.

5.9.3 Precedence

The operators $\square$ and $\diamond$ are unary and cannot express properties that relate two points in time, such as the *precedence* property that requires that A become true before B becomes true. This can be expressed with the binary operator $\mathcal{U}$ called *until* and written U in SPIN:

$$\neg B \, \mathcal{U} \, A.$$

Read this as: B remains false until A becomes true. More formally:

> $p \, \mathcal{U} \, q$ is true in state s_i of a computation τ if and only if there is some state s_k in τ with $k \geq i$, such that q is true in s_k, and for all s_j in τ such that $i \leq j < k$, p is true in s_j.

If q is already true in s_i, the second requirement is vacuous.

The formula $\neg B \, \mathcal{U} \, A$ is true in s_0 of the following computation because B remains false as long as A does; only in s_4, when A becomes true, does B also become true:

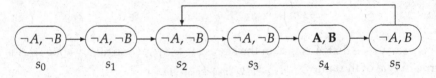

Note that B need not be true in s_4, because we are only interested in specifying that it remain false until A becomes true. In fact, B can be false throughout the entire computation, and the truth of A beyond its first true occurrence is irrelevant; it follows that $\neg B \, \mathcal{U} \, A$ is true in s_0 of the following computation:

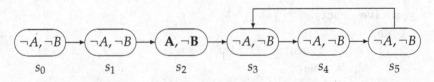

The operator $\mathcal{U}$ is called the *strong until* operator, because the subformula to the right of $\mathcal{U}$ is required to become true eventually. In fact $\diamond q$ can be defined as *true* $\mathcal{U} q$. Since *true* is trivially true, *true* $\mathcal{U} q$ is true if and only if q eventually becomes true.

There is a *weak until* operator $\mathcal{W}$ that does not require that the right subformula eventually become true. The two operators are related as follows:

$$pUq \equiv pWq \wedge \Diamond q, \qquad pWq \equiv pUq \vee \Box p.$$

Warning

SPIN does not have the weak until operator W.

Advanced: The V operator

SPIN has an operator V that is defined so that pVq is equivalent to
`!( (!p) U (!q) )`. The operator V is *not* the same as W; if it were,
the corresponding formula would be `!( (!q) U (!p && !q) )`.

5.9.4 Overtaking

We will demonstrate the use of the U operator to specify *one-bounded over-taking* in Peterson's algorithm (Listing 5.4), a correct solution to the critical section problem. One-bounded overtaking means that if process P tries to enter its critical section, process Q can enter its critical section at most once before P does.

Let us define the symbols:

```
#define    ptry    P@try
#define    qcs     Q@cs
#define    pcs     P@cs
```

If process P is not in its critical section, it is *not* true that csq is false, and it is certainly not true that csq remains false until P enters its critical section. First, process Q may currently be in its critical section, but even if it isn't, it may *overtake* process P and enter its critical section first.

One-bounded overtaking is expressed by the LTL formula [17, p. 265]:

```
[]( ptry -> ( !qcs U ( qcs U (!qcs U pcs) ) ) )
```

A nested *until* formula of this form expresses the property that a sequence of intervals must satisfy successive subformula. The formula above expresses the property that, *always*, if process P is trying to enter its critical section (ptry is true), the computation must start with the following sequence of intervals: (a) process Q is not in its critical section (!qcs); (b) process Q is in its critical section (qcs); (c) again, process Q is not in its critical section (!qcs); and finally (d) process P is in its critical section (pcs).

According to the definition of the U operator, the intervals may be empty, but the correctness of this property ensures that there cannot be two *separate* intervals where qcs is true before the state where pcs becomes true.

Run a verification of the program in Listing 5.4 for this formula and show that one-bounded overtaking holds.

Listing 5.4. Peterson's algorithm

```
1  bool  wantP, wantQ;
2  byte  last = 1;
3
4  active proctype P() {
5    do
6    ::  wantP = true;
7        last = 1;
8  try:  (wantQ == false) || (last == 2);
9  cs:   wantP = false
10   od
11 }
12
13 active proctype Q() {
14   do
15   ::  wantQ = true;
16       last = 2;
17 try:  (wantP == false) || (last == 1);
18 cs:   wantQ = false
19   od
20 }
```

Warning

The operator U is defined in SPIN to be left-associative, while the operator $\mathcal{U}$ is defined to be right-associative in [17, p. 48], the definitive reference on linear temporal logic. Right-associativity is more natural because it corresponds to a sequence of intervals, as explained in [17].

To avoid confusion, use parentheses liberally!

Advanced: Bounded overtaking with weak until

Normally, one-bounded overtaking would be verified using a for-
mula with the weak until operator $\mathcal{W}$ rather than $\mathcal{U}$. This is because in
the critical section problem a process need not attempt to execute its
critical section, so csq may never become true. Since $\mathcal{W}$ is not implemented in SPIN, we have used $\mathcal{U}$; the verification still works because
the algorithm in Listing 5.4 does not model a process that remains in
its noncritical section.

5.9.5 Next

Temporal logic contains an additional unary operator $\mathcal{X}$, called *next* and
written X in SPIN. $\mathcal{X}A$ is true in a state s_i of a computation if A is true in
the following state s_{i+1}. The operator is of limited usefulness for two rea-
sons. First, the usual model of a concurrent or distributed system abstracts
away from the concept of time. For example, in a client-server system, we
want to specify that a client process *eventually* receives a service from a server
process, but it doesn't really matter if that occurs in the next state or ten
states later. The modeling of real-time systems in which time does matter is
discussed in the case studies in Sections 11.3 and 11.4.

The second reason for avoiding $\mathcal{X}$ is that without this operator temporal
logic formulas are *stutter invariant*. This means that any correctness specification that is true in a computation remains true if duplicate consecutive states
are removed to form a more concise computation. The algorithms in SPIN
are more efficient if stutter-invariant specifications are used. In fact you may
have noticed the following message from SPIN:

```
warning: for p.o. reduction to be valid
    the never claim must be stutter-invariant
(never claims generated from LTL formulae
 . are stutter-invariant)
```

p.o. reduction refers to *partial order reduction*, which is one of the main optimizations that SPIN is able to perform (Section 10.2.) As the last lines of
the message note, if you limit yourself to writing correctness specifications
in LTL, you need not worry about affecting this optimization.

For more on these topics see *SMC* Chapter 6.

Data and Program Structures

As we have noted more than once, PROMELA is designed for modeling a system, not for implementing one with an executable program. Typically, a model will be relatively small in size, so that it will be feasible to verify correctness properties by searching its state space. A model with a handful of variables and two dozen statements can give rise to complex behavior that strains the model-checking abilities of SPIN. For that reason PROMELA does not include an extensive set of constructs for structuring the program and its data; in particular, you will not find constructs like functions and classes that facilitate the development of large programs. PROMELA does have arrays and type definitions that are used for structuring data, and it has macros and inline declarations that can help make programs more readable.

6.1 Arrays

In common with almost all programming languages, PROMELA includes the *array* – a sequence of data values of the same type whose elements can be accessed by providing an index giving the position of the element within the sequence. The syntax and semantics of arrays are similar to those of C-like languages; the first position in the array is at index zero and square brackets are used for the indexing operation. It is an error if the index is not within the bounds of an array: An error message will be printed during simulation (without terminating the computation) and the error will be reported when it is encountered during verification.

Arrays in PROMELA are one-dimensional; a workaround to this limitation is presented in the next section.

Listing 6.1 shows a program to compute the sum of the elements of an array of values of type **int**. The array a is declared and initialized by a sequence

Listing 6.1. Computing the sum of the elements of an array of integer type

```
1   #include "for.h"
2   active proctype P() {
3     int a[5];
4     a[0] = 0; a[1] = 10; a[2] = 20; a[3] = 30; a[4] = 40;
5     int sum = 0;
6     for (i, 0, 4)
7       sum = sum + a[i]
8     rof (i);
9     printf("The sum of the numbers = %d\n", sum)
10  }
```

of assignment statements; then a counting loop is used to compute the sum of the elements. The elements of an array can be initialized by a computation from within a loop:

```
for (j, 0, 4)
  a[j] = j * 10
rof (j)
```

perhaps by a nondeterministic expression:

```
for (j, 0, 4)
  if
  :: a[j] = j * 10
  :: a[j] = j + 5
  fi
rof (j)
```

An initial value in a declaration is assigned to all the elements of the array:

```
int a[5] = 10;
```

Warning

Arrays of type **bit** or **bool** are stored as arrays of type **byte**. If you have a large array of bits and need to save memory, you can encode them in bytes using shift and mask. An example of this is given in Section 11.7.2.

6.2 Type definitions

Compound types are defined with **typedef** and are primarily used for defining the structure of messages to be sent over channels:

```
typedef MESSAGE {
  mtype message;
  byte source;
  byte destination;
  bool urgent
}
```

This point will be discussed further in Chapter 7.

An additional use of type definitions is to work around the PROMELA limitation to one-dimensional arrays. A two-dimensional array is declared as an array whose elements are of a type defined by a type definition with a single array field:

```
typedef VECTOR {
  int vector[10]
}
VECTOR matrix[5];
  ...
matrix[3].vector[6] = matrix[4].vector[7];
```

The syntax is the same as in C-like languages: brackets are used for indexing an array and a dot for selecting a field within a compound type.

Listing 6.2 shows a program that uses type definitions to initialize and print a sparse array.[1] A *sparse array* is a data structure used to store an array most of whose elements are known to be zero. For each nonzero element of the array, its row, column, and value are stored. The program creates a data structure for a sparse array and then prints out the entire array as a matrix of rows and columns. It assumes that the elements are stored in lexicographic order of the rows and columns.

The type definition ENTRY (lines 3–7) declares a structure of a single element of a sparse array; the elements are stored in an array a whose elements are of this type (line 8). Since it is not possible to assign a value of a defined type to a variable of the type, we have to initialize the data structure field by field (lines 12–15). (See Section 6.4 for a more readable way of doing this.)

The sparse array is printed within nested loops (lines 17–28), the outer one for the rows and the inner one for the columns. The local variable i is used as an index into the data structure that holds the elements of the sparse

---

[1] See also the implementation of sparse arrays in the case study in Section 11.1.

Listing 6.2. Data structure for a sparse array

```
1   #include "for.h"
2   #define N 4
3   typedef ENTRY {
4     byte row;
5     byte col;
6     int value
7   }
8   ENTRY a[N];
9
10  active proctype P() {
11    int i = 0;
12    a[0].row = 0; a[0].col = 1; a[0].value = -5;
13    a[1].row = 0; a[1].col = 3; a[1].value = 8;
14    a[2].row = 2; a[2].col = 0; a[2].value = 20;
15    a[3].row = 3; a[3].col = 3; a[3].value = -3;
16
17    for (r, 0, N-1)
18      for (c, 0, N-1)
19        if
20        :: i == N -> printf("0 ")
21        :: i < N && r == a[i].row && c == a[i].col ->
22             printf("%d ", a[i].value);
23             i++
24        :: else -> printf("0 ")
25        fi
26      rof (c);
27      printf("\n")
28    rof (r)
29  }
```

array. The **if**-statement for printing a single element has three alternatives: (1) The first alternative (line 20) is used when we have printed out all non-zero elements of the array, in which case the remaining elements are zero. (2) The second alternative (lines 21–23) checks if the values of the loop variables are equal to the row and column values of the current element of the sparse array; if so, the value stored in the element is printed. (3) Otherwise, a zero is printed in the third alternative (line 24). The output of this program is:

0	-5	0	8
0	0	0	0
20	0	0	0
0	0	0	-3

The columns are not aligned because some numbers need two characters on output. PROMELA does not support width specifiers as does C.

6.3 The preprocessor

SPIN is implemented in C, a language that not contain a mechanism for structuring programs into modules; instead, interface declarations are contained within files that are included within the source files that form the program. Inclusion of source code is implemented by a compile-time software tool called the *preprocessor*, which is called before the compiler itself is executed. The preprocessor is also used to conduct text-based macro processing on the source code. *Text-based* means that the preprocessor has no knowledge of the syntax and semantics of the language, but instead treats the source code as pure text.

When SPIN is run in any mode, it first calls a preprocessor, which is normally the same as the preprocessor associated with the compiler used to compile the verifiers. We have already seen the use of the preprocessor to include a file:

```
#include "for.h"
```

and to declare a symbol:

```
#define N 4
```

Declaring a symbol does not use memory because the definition is simply substituted for the symbol before SPIN simulates the program or generates the code for the verifier.

#define is also used for declaring symbols for expressions used in correctness specifications (Chapter 5):

```
#define mutex (critical <= 1)
```

The next two subsections survey advanced features of the preprocessor, though in most cases, **#define**, **#include**, and the **inline** construct described in the next section will be sufficient for writing models.

6.3.1 Condition compilation*

The preprocessor can be used to implement *conditional compilation*, which enables the compile-time parameterization of a program. Suppose that a model is to be verified under several different assumptions, for example, under three different priority schemes. The following preprocessor code enables different expressions to be used for the variable currentPriority simply by defining one of the symbols VerOne, VerTwo, or VerThree with **#define** at the beginning of the program:

```
#ifdef VerOne
  currentPriority = (p1 > p2 -> p1 : p2);
#endif
#ifdef VerTwo
  currentPriority = PMAX;
#endif
#ifdef VerThree
  currentPriority = PMIN;
#endif
```

Symbols can also be defined using the –D argument on the SPIN command; so, for example,

```
spin -DVerTwo pri.pml
```

would run SPIN on this program with the symbol VerTwo defined and thus currentPriority set to PMAX. This is particularly useful when verifications are run from a script, so that you do not have to edit the PROMELA source code.

Another technique that can be used instead of conditional compilation is to write a program (in any language) to generate PROMELA code for different versions of the model. This is used, for example, in the software tool VN, where a program written in JAVA generates PROMELA programs for finite automata (Section 8.2).

6.3.2 Macros*

#define is not limited to simple textual substitution of a string for a single symbol; it can be used to create macros that can improve the readability of PROMELA programs. For example, the macros for counting loops (Section 1.7.1) are defined as follows:

```
#define for(I,low,high) \
    byte I; \
    I = low ; \
    do \
    :: ( I > high ) -> break \
    :: else ->

#define rof(I) \
    ; I++ \
    od
```

The backslash character denotes that the substitution text for the macro is continued on the next line. Alternatively, you can define the entire macro on one line.

Be careful what actual parameters you give when calling the macro. Clearly, these macros are intended to be used with a variable name substituted for I. If by chance you call the for macro with j+1 as the first parameter, you will get weird error messages caused by SPIN trying to decipher:

```
byte j+1;
```

Advanced: Debugging and changing the preprocessor

To debug macros, run SPIN with the argument -I; this will write to standard output the results of performing the preprocessing.

You can use an alternate preprocessor by calling SPIN with the argument -P. This argument is also useful for giving the full path of the preprocessor if SPIN cannot find it.

SPIN performs some elementary preprocessing operations itself, for example, the replacement of defined symbols; therefore, problems accessing the preprocessor will not manifest themselves unless advanced preprocessing features are used.

6.4 Inline

Although PROMELA does not have functions or procedures for structuring code, it can be convenient to group statements together so that they can appear in several places in a program. This is done using the **inline** construct, which gives a name to a sequence of statements. Listing 6.3 shows the use of **inline** to write a "procedure" for printing the elements of an array.[2] When-

---

[2] The sequence of statements is contained within **d_step** because there is no meaning to the internal states of the sequence and the statements can be executed deterministically.

ever the name of the inlined sequence is used within a **proctype**, the statements between the braces are copied to the corresponding position before compilation.

During the copy the formal parameters appearing after the name of the inlined sequence are replaced by the actual parameters of the call. There is no type declaration associated with the formal parameter because textual substitution is performed without any syntactical or semantic checking whatsoever. Any problems caused by the substitution will only be found during the subsequent compilation of the resulting PROMELA source code.

Listing 6.3. Printing an array with **inline**

```
1   #include "for.h"
2   #define N 5
3
4   inline write(ar) {
5     d_step {
6       for (k, 0, N-1)
7         printf("%d ", ar[k])
8       rof (k);
9       printf("\n")
10    }
11  }
12
13  active proctype P() {
14    int a[N];
15    write(a);
16    for (i, 0, N-1)
17      a[i] = i
18    rof (i);
19    write(a)
20  }
```

inline is useful for initializing data structures. The readability of the program for sparse arrays in Listing 6.2 can be improved by declaring an **inline** for the initialization of the entries:

```
inline initEntry(I, R, C, V) {
  a[I].row = R;
  a[I].col = C;
  a[I].value = V;
}
```

The statements for initializing the values of the array are now much easier to write and read:

```
initEntry(0, 0, 1, -5);
initEntry(1, 0, 3, 8);
initEntry(2, 2, 0, 20);
initEntry(3, 3, 3, -3);
```

Warning

No new scope is created for an inline sequence!

Any variables declared within the sequence are equivalent to local variables declared directly within the **proctype** where the sequence is called.

SPIN will print an error message when compiling the program in Listing 6.3 because both calls of the inline write declare the loop variable k. The message can be ignored. Alternatively, the for-macro can be redefined not to declare the variable, in which case the calling process becomes responsible for its declaration.

Advanced: Inline vs. macros

The **inline** construct in SPIN is almost identical to the macro construct, but its syntax is more "friendly" because there is no need to use continuation characters. In addition, errors will be reported with the line number within the **inline** construct, rather than with the line of the call.

Channels

Distributed systems are computer systems consisting of a set of *nodes* connected by *communications channels*. The most familiar distributed system is, of course, the Internet, which consists of millions of computers connected by communications networks implemented with wires, optical fibers and microwave radio. *Protocols* such as TCP/IP and HTTP define how data are moved between nodes of the network. The network itself is quite complex, using computers to perform essential communications functions such as routing, name lookup, and error correction. To model a distributed system we abstract away details of the network and its protocols, and model nodes as concurrent processes and communications networks as channels over which processes can send and receive messages.

The most widely used formalism for modeling distributed systems is called *Communicating Sequential Processes (CSP)*, after a 1978 article by that name, written by C.A.R. Hoare [11]. CSP was the inspiration for the communications constructs in several programming languages such as OCCAM and ADA, as well as for the channel construct in PROMELA.

Warning

In CSP and OCCAM a channel is always associated with a pair of processes; that is, exactly one process can send to each channel and exactly one process can receive from a channel. In PROMELA channels are global entities not associated with processes, so any process can send a message on any channel and receive a message from any channel. In fact, a process can send messages to and receive messages from a single channel!

Throughout this chapter we will use a *client-server system* as a running example. A number of processes called *clients* send *requests* to other processes called *servers*. A server performs a service and can return a *result* to a client.

Since there are quite a few programs in this chapter for the client-server example, we suggest that – while you read the text – you run simulations and verifications on the source code from the software archives.

Channels are used extensively in the case studies in Chapter 11. For other examples of distributed systems see *SMC*, which uses a telephone exchange as its running example. There, channels model the communications lines between telephone subscribers and the exchange, and between the exchanges themselves.

7.1 Channels in PROMELA

A *channel* in PROMELA is a data type with two operations, *send* and *receive*. Every channel has associated with it a *message type*; once a channel has been initialized, it can only send and receive messages of its message type. At most 255 channels can be created.

Listing 7.1 shows a model of a client-server system, where two clients are connected to a single server through a channel called request. The channel is declared with an *initializer* specifying the *channel capacity* and the message type:

chan ch = [capacity] **of** { typename, ..., typename }

The channel capacity must be a nonnegative integer constant. The message type specifies the structure of each message that can be sent on the channel as a sequence of fields; the number of fields and the type of each field are specified in the declaration. In the program in Listing 7.1, the capacity of the channel is zero, while the message type consists of a single field of type **byte**.

There are two types of channels with different semantics: *rendezvous* channels of capacity zero and *buffered channels* of capacity greater than zero. In subsequent sections we will discuss these separately.

Warning

The type of a message field cannot be an array; however, the type can be a **typedef** (Section 6.2) and the **typedef** can contain an array.

Syntactically, the *send statement* consists of a channel variable followed by an exclamation point and then a sequence of *expressions* whose number and

Listing 7.1. Client-server using channels

```
1  chan request = [0] of { byte };
2
3  active proctype Server() {
4    byte client;
5  end:
6    do
7    :: request ? client ->
8         printf("Client %d\n", client)
9    od
10 }
11
12 active proctype Client0() {
13   request ! 0
14 }
15
16 active proctype Client1() {
17   request ! 1
18 }
```

types match the message type of the channel. The *receive statement* consists of a channel variable followed by question mark and a sequence of *variables*.[1]

Semantically, the expressions in the send statement are evaluated and their values are transferred through the channel; the receive statement assigns these values to the variables listed in the statement.

In the program in Listing 7.1, each client sents an integer value on the channel (lines 13, 17); the server receives the values and assigns them to the variable client (line 7).

Clearly, a receive statement cannot be executable unless a message is available in the channel. Receive statements will frequently appear as guards in an **if**- or **do**-statement, as shown in line 7 of Listing 7.1.

Note the use of the end label in the server; while it is reasonable for client processes to send a number of requests and then terminate, a server process never knows when it will be called upon to process a request, so it should never terminate. The label ensures that an end state with the server blocked on a receive statement is not considered invalid (see Section 4.7).

---

[1] See Section 7.5 for the use of values and expressions in receive statements.

A bit of syntactic sugar for send and receive statements is supported: the list of expressions ch!e1,e2,... can be written: ch!e1(e2,...). This is primarily used when the first argument is an **mtype**, indicating the type of the message. For example, given the declarations:

```
mtype { open, close, reset };
chan ch = [1] of { mtype, byte, byte };
byte id, n;
```

a send statement can be written in either of the following formats:

```
ch ! open, id, n;
ch ! open(id, n);
```

7.1.1 Channels and channel variables

The type of all channel variables is **chan** and a channel variable holds a reference or "handle" to the channel itself, which is created by an initializer. This means that channel variables can appear in assignment statements or, more commonly, as parameters to a **proctype** or **inline**:

```
chan ch1 = [0] of { byte };
chan ch2 = [0] of { byte, byte };
proctype P(chan c) {
  c ! 5
}
init {
  run P(ch1);
  run P(ch2)
}
```

Since the message in a send statement must match the message type of the channel, the send in the second instantiation of P causes a runtime, but not a compile-time, error, demonstrating that the channel *variable* is not typed with a message type.[2]

A channel can be sent in a message and received by another process; see Listing 7.5 for an example.

Advanced: Local channels

Channels are usually initialized globally, though one can be declared and initialized locally and then passed to another process in a message. However, if a channel is declared and initialized within a process and the process then dies, the channel is no longer accessible.

---

[2] The error is currently not reported but this will be fixed in Version 5 of SPIN.

Listing 7.2. Simple program with rendezvous

```
1   mtype { red, yellow, green };
2   chan ch = [0] of { mtype, byte, bool };
3
4   active proctype Sender() {
5     ch ! red, 20, false;
6     printf("Sent message\n")
7   }
8
9   active proctype Receiver() {
10    mtype color;
11    byte time;
12    bool flash;
13    ch ? color, time, flash;
14    printf("Received message %e, %d, %d\n",
15          color, time, flash)
16  }
```

7.2 Rendezvous channels

A channel declared with a capacity of zero is a *rendezvous channel*. This means that the transfer of the message from the *sender* (a process with a send statement) to the *receiver* (a process with a receive statement) is *synchronous* and is executed as a single atomic operation. For the program in Listing 7.2, the atomic transfer is suggested by the arrow in the following diagram that goes directly from the send statement to the receive statement, so that there is no state between sending and receiving:

```
        Sender                              Receiver
          ⋮                                    ⋮
(green,20,false) ─────────────────→ (color,time,flash)
          ⋮                                    ⋮
```

When the location counter of the sender is at the send statement (line 5), it is said to *offer* to engage in a rendezvous. If the location counter of the receiver is at the matching receive statement (line 13), the rendezvous can be *accepted* and the values of the data in the send statement are copied to the variables in the receive statement. The state change is shown in the following diagram:

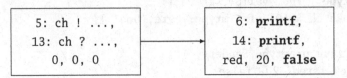

```
5: ch ! ...,              6: printf,
13: ch ? ...,            14: printf,
   0, 0, 0            red, 20, false
```

In the state on the left, the location counter of process Sender is at the send statement in line 5, while the location counter of process Receiver is at the receive statement in line 13. The rendezvous that is offered by Sender can be accepted by Receiver. The state that results from executing the rendezvous is shown on the right. The location counters of *both* processes are incremented, and, in addition, the values in the send statement are transferred to the corresponding variables in the receive statement. The rendezvous is one *atomic* operation; even if there were other processes, no interleaving could take place between the execution of the send statement and the receive statement.

A send statement that offers to engage in a rendezvous for which there is no matching receive statement is itself not executable, and similarly for an executable receive statement with no matching executable send statement. The process containing such a statement is blocked (unless, of course, there are alternatives with true guards in an **if**- or **do**-statement).

In the client-server program in Listing 7.1, any of the three processes can be executed first. If the client processes execute first, they will block on their send statements request!0 (line 13) and request!1 (line 17) until the matching receive statement in the server request?client (line 7) is executable. Since both clients offer to engage in the rendezvous before the server executes the receive statement, the choice between the two send statements is made nondeterministically: randomly in random simulation mode, and in verification mode, both choices are searched.

Similarly, if the server attempts to execute the receive statement before either client offers to engage in a rendezvous, it is blocked. Since there are no other alternatives in its **do**-statement, the entire process is blocked.

7.2.1 Reply channels

The program in Listing 7.1 is unrealistic because the clients receive no results from the server, not even acknowledgements that the service has been successfully carried out. Listing 7.3 shows a program with an additional channel reply used by the server to return an acknowledgement to a client after performing the service. Note the use of the *anonymous variable* denoted by an underscore in lines 16 and 21; we are interested only in the receipt of the

Listing 7.3. Client-server with a reply channel

```
1  chan request = [0] of { byte };
2  chan reply = [0] of { bool };
3
4  active proctype Server() {
5    byte client;
6  end:
7    do,
8    :: request ? client ->
9           printf("Client %d\n", client);
10          reply ! true
11   od
12 }
13
14 active proctype Client0() {
15   request ! 0;
16   reply ? _
17 }
18
19 active proctype Client1() {
20   request ! 1;
21   reply ? _
22 }
```

message and not in its content, which is uniformly true. (Another example of the use of the anonymous variable is given in Section 9.2.1.)

There is still a lack of realism in the program because, typically, there are several servers that can service requests from a set of clients. Listing 7.4 shows a program with two servers and two clients; we have used the process identifier _pid to identify both the clients and the servers.

Unfortunately, this program is not correct. The model is faithful to the concept that the two servers should be independent of each other, as should the two clients. However, we need to ensure that the client receiving the reply sent by the server in line 11 is the same as the client who sent the request that was received by the server in line 8. A few random simulations of the program gave the following output that shows that each client received the reply intended for the other:

Listing 7.4. Multiple clients and servers

```
1  chan request = [0] of { byte };
2  chan reply = [0] of { byte };
3
4  active [2] proctype Server() {
5    byte client;
6  end:
7    do
8    :: request ? client ->
9         printf("Client %d processed by server %d\n",
10                client, _pid);
11         reply ! _pid
12    od
13  }
14
15  active [2] proctype Client() {
16    byte server;
17    request ! _pid;
18    reply ? server;
19    printf("Reply received from server %d by client %d\n",
20            server, _pid)
21  }
```

```
Client 2 processed by server 1
Reply received from server 1 by client 3
Client 3 processed by server 0
Reply received from server 0 by client 2
```

The error can also be found by attempting to verify the program. Modify line 11 so that the server returns to the client the ID that it received:

```
reply ! _pid, client;
```

Declare an additional local variable whichClient in each client to receive the second message field sent by the server (line 18):

```
reply ? server, whichClient;
```

Now, add after line 20 an assertion that checks that the ID received from the server is same as the _pid of the client that sent the request:

```
assert (whichClient == _pid);
```

Listing 7.5. An array of channels

```
1  chan request = [0] of { byte, chan };
2  chan reply [2] = [0] of { byte, byte };
3
4  active [2] proctype Server() {
5    byte client;
6    chan replyChannel;
7  end:
8    do
9    :: request ? client, replyChannel ->
10       printf("Client %d processed by server %d\n",
11             client, _pid);
12       replyChannel ! _pid, client
13    od
14  }
15
16  active [2] proctype Client() {
17    byte server;
18    byte whichClient;
19    request ! _pid, reply[_pid-2];
20    reply[_pid-2] ? server, whichClient;
21    printf("Reply received from server %d by client %d\n",
22          server, _pid);
23    assert(whichClient == _pid)
24  }
```

SPIN quickly locates a computation that violates the assertion:

```
pan: assertion violated (whichClient==_pid) (at depth 8)
```

7.2.2 Arrays of channels

One way to fix the above error is to associate a separate reply channel with each client. Listing 7.5 is similar to Listing 7.4 with several changes:

- The reply channel is changed to be an array of two channels (line 2), one for each client.
- The messages on the request channels include a field of type **chan** for the reply channel in addition to the field of type **byte** for the client ID (line 1).

- A client sends the reply channel associated with it (in addition to its ID) (line 19) and a server receives the value and stores it in the variable replyChannel (line 20).
- The server uses the received value of the reply channel to ensure that the reply is sent to the correct client (line 12).
- The client waits for a reply on the channel associated with it (line 20).

Running a verification in SPIN shows that the assertion is never violated.

This program emphasizes that there is nothing special about channel values; they are only handles to the actual channel created in the initializer.

The use of _pid-2 to obtain the index of the channel in the client processess (lines 19–20) is not a robust programming technique, because the _pid will change if an additional process is declared before the client processes. The software archive contains a version of this program where the IDs and indices are passed as parameters of a **run** operator, and thus are less likely to need modification.

7.2.3 Local channels

Rather than using a global array of channels, each client can declare its own local channel. Delete line 2 in Listing 7.5 and replace lines 19–20 of the client processes with

```
chan reply = [0] of { byte, byte };
request ! _pid, reply;
reply ? server, whichClient;
```

The channel will disappear when the client process dies.

7.2.4 Limitations of rendezvous channels

Normally, there are many more clients than servers. Think of well known websites for search engines and online stores. They may have dozens or even hundreds of servers, but they must serve requests from thousands of clients simultaneously. If rendezvous channels were used, the number of clients actually being served can be no larger than the number of servers, so the rest of the clients would be blocked. We can show this by counting the number of clients in our program that have successfully sent the request but have yet to receive the reply. With two servers and four clients, there can be at most two clients in this state.

To see this, add a global variable numClients to the program in Listing 7.5; the variable will count the number of clients that have sent a request but have yet to receive the result from the server. Replace the code for the client process by

```
active [4] proctype Client() {
    byte server;
    request ! _pid, reply[_pid-2];
    numClients++;
    assert (numClients <= 2);
    numClients--;
    reply[_pid-2] ? server
}
```

When a verification is performed, no errors are found, indicating that at most two out of the four clients have reached that control point. The other two are potentially blocked on the send statement.

7.3 Buffered channels

The solution to the problem in the previous section is to queue the requests for service sent by the client in such a way that they do not block either the client or the server.

A channel declared with a positive capacity is called a *buffered channel*:

```
chan ch = [3] of { mtype, byte, bool };
```

The capacity is the number of messages of the message type that can be stored in the channel. The following diagram is similar to the one shown in Section 7.2 for the program in Listing 7.2 except that a buffered channel is used:

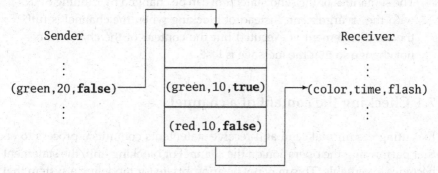

The send and receive statements treat the channel as a FIFO (first in-first out) queue. (Other versions of the send and receive statements are described Sections 7.5–7.8.) The diagram shows the channel as it would appear if two messages have already been sent to the channel; more precisely, it shows the channel after two *more* messages have been sent than have been received. The send statement is executable because there is room in the channel for another message, that is, the channel is *not full*; executing the statement places the message at the tail of the queue. The receive statement is executable because there are messages in the channel, that is, the channel is *not empty*; executing the statement removes the message at the head of the queue and assigns its values to the variables in the receive command.

The channel is part of the states of the computation. The send and receive statements are each executed atomically. The state diagram corresponding to the one on page 110 is:

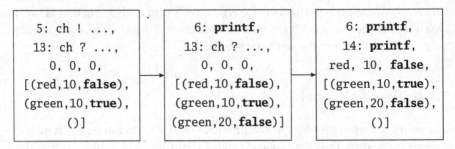

The channel is shown as a triple [_,_,_] with space for three elements.

If we change the program in Listing 7.5 to use a buffered channel of capacity 4 and rerun the verification of the program described at the end of Section 7.2.4, SPIN will find a computation in which numClients <= 2 is falsified, as we would expect since none of the four senders can ever be blocked.

Another solution to this problem is given in Section 7.5.

Advanced: Lost messages when the channel is full

The semantics of the send statement can be changed by running SPIN with the -m argument. Instead of blocking when the channel is full, the send statement is executed but the content of the channel does not change so that the message is lost.

7.4 Checking the content of a channel

Executing the normal send and receive statements commits a process to either performing the operation on the channel or blocking until the statement becomes executable. This may not be appropriate for modeling a system that can perform other tasks when a channel operation is not executable.

> ## Warning
>
> The functions described in this section are allowed only for buffered channels, because it makes no sense to talk about "the number of messages" in a rendezvous channel.

7.4.1 Checking if a channel is full or empty

There are four predefined boolean functions for checking a channel: **full** and **empty**, and their negations **nfull** and **nempty**.

> ## Warning
>
> The negations !**full** and !**empty** are not allowed in PROMELA, so **nfull** and **nempty** must be used instead. The predefined functions may unintentionally become negated in a never claim; if so, you should modify the code of the claim itself.

Suppose that neither the clients nor the servers in the system should be blocked on a channel; that is, the client should be able to do another computation if a channel is full, and, similarly, the server should be able to do another computation if the channel is empty. This system is modeled in the program in Listing 7.6, where "another computation" is modeled by the **printf** statements in lines 9 and 21. The predefined boolean functions **nfull** and **empty** are used in the guards of the **do**-statements to provide an executable alternative if the send or receive statements are not executable.[3]

> ## Warning
>
> Do not use **else** alternatives in **if**- or **do**-statements that have channel expressions as their guards; instead, use the pairs **empty/nempty** and **full/nfull**.

7.4.2 Checking the number of messages in a channel

There is a predefined integer function **len**(ch) that returns the number of messages in channel ch. This is less useful than it may seem at first glance because most models need only check the extreme cases of **len**(ch)==0 and **len**(ch)==N (where N is the capacity of ch), for which the functions of the previous subsection suffice. One example of its use is in a model of process

---

[3] We have removed the end label because the program is nonterminating.

Listing 7.6. Checking if the channel is full or empty

```
1  chan request = [2] of { byte, chan};
2  chan reply[2] = [2] of { byte };
3
4  active [2] proctype Server() {
5    byte client;
6    chan replyChannel;
7    do
8    :: empty(request) ->
9        printf("No requests for server %d\n", _pid)
10   :: request ? client, replyChannel ->
11       printf("Client %d processed by server %d\n",
12             client, _pid);
13       replyChannel ! _pid
14   od
15 }
16
17 active [2] proctype Client() {
18   byte server;
19   do
20   :: nfull(request) ->
21       printf("Client %d waiting for non-full channel\n",
22             _pid);
23   :: request ! _pid, reply[_pid-2] ->
24       reply[_pid-2] ? server;
25       printf("Reply received from server %d by client %d\n",
26             server, _pid)
27   od
28 }
```

allocation: when the channel is more than three-quarters full, allocate more
server processes to service the overload, and when the channel is less than
one-quarter full, some processors can be deallocated:

```
if
:: len(ch) > (3*N/4) -> /* Allocate a new server */
:: len(ch) < (N/4)   -> /* Deallocate a server */
:: else
fi
```

Use the functions **empty, nempty, full, nfull** instead of **len** whenever possible, because they can be used by the SPIN optimization called partial order reduction (Section 10.2) to improve the efficiency of verifications.

7.5 Random receive*

Buffered channels can be used to implement a different solution to the client-server problem (Listing 7.7), in which the array of four reply channels has been replaced by a single channel of capacity four (line 2). The message sent on the reply channel (line 11) contains the server ID, as well as the ID of the client that was received from the request channel (line 8). We need to ensure that it is possible for a client to receive only messages meant for it, but this cannot be done with the channel statements as we have defined them so far.

Listing 7.7. Random receive from a buffered channel

```
1   chan request = [4] of { byte };
2   chan reply = [4] of { byte, byte };
3
4   active [2] proctype Server() {
5     byte client;
6   end:
7     do
8     :: request ? client ->
9          printf("Client %d processed by server %d\n",
10                 client, _pid);
11         reply ! _pid, client
12    od
13  }
14
15  active [4] proctype Client() {
16    byte server;
17    request ! _pid;
18    reply ?? server, eval(_pid);
19    printf("Reply received from server %d by client %d\n",
20           server, _pid)
21  }
```

The first problem is that channels are FIFO, so even if a channel contains a message for a certain client, the client cannot receive the message until all messages ahead of it in the queue have been removed from the channel. To solve this problem we can use the PROMELA statement called *random receive*, which receives messages from *anywhere* within the channel, not just at the head; it is denoted by the double question mark as shown in line 18.

The second problem is that the receive statement removes a message regardless of its content and assigns the values to the variables in the statement. Here it is required that a client remove only messages intended for itself. To solve this problem the receive statement allows *values* to be used instead of variables. A receive statement is executable if and only if its variables and values *match* the values in the fields of a message. A variable matches any field whose value is of the correct type, but a value matches a field if and only if it equals the value of the field. When the message is received, it is removed from the channel and values are assigned to the variables in the statement; of course, there is no meaning to assigning values to values.

A random receive statement will remove the *first* message that matches the variables and values in the statement. If the value to be matched is known when the program is written (for example, the client ID is a constant), it can be used directly:

```
reply ?? server, 3
```

But sometimes the value is known only at runtime, for example, when it is the value of a parameter to the **proctype**, or, as in this case, when it is the value of **_pid** that is different for each instantiation of the **proctype**. In these cases, **eval** is used to obtain *the current value of the variable* to use in the matching (line 18):

```
reply ?? server, eval(_pid)
```

This ensures that only messages intended for this client are matched and are removed from the channel.

The name "random receive" is misleading because there is nothing at all that is random or even nondeterministic about the statement: it is executable if a matching message exists, and if it is executed, the first matching message is received.

Another example of the use of random receive is given in Section 11.3.

Listing 7.8. Storing values in sorted order

```
1   chan ch = [3] of { byte };
2
3   inline getValue() {
4     if
5     :: n = 1
6     :: n = 2
7     :: n = 3
8     fi
9   }
10
11  active proctype Sort() {
12    byte n;
13    getValue();
14    ch !! n;
15    getValue();
16    ch !! n;
17    getValue();
18    ch !! n;
19    ch ? n;
20    printf("%d\n", n);
21    ch ? n;
22    printf("%d\n", n);
23    ch ? n;
24    printf("%d\n", n)
25  }
```

7.6 Sorted send*

A send statement for a buffered channel inserts the message at the tail of
the message queue in the channel. With the *sorted send* statement, written
ch!!message with a double exclamation point, the message is inserted *ahead*
of the first message that is larger than it. Fields of the message are interpreted
as integer values, and if there are multiple fields, lexicographic ordering is
used. Sorted send can be used to model a data structure such as a priority
queue. The program in Listing 7.8 prints three values in sorted order, even
though they are generated nondeterministically. For another example of the
use of sorted send, see Section 11.3.

7.7 Copying the value of a message*

Sometimes we are interested in copying the values in a message without removing the message from the channel. The following statements copy the values of a message into the three variables but does not remove it:

```
ch ? <color, time, flash>
ch ?? <color, time, flash>
```

This statement is distinguished from normal and random receive statements by the use of angle brackets to enclose a list of variables. Copying without removing is useful when channels are used to implement data structures, as described in Section 11.1.

7.8 Polling*

Real-time systems are built in two architectural styles:

- In an interrupt-driven system, a sensor causes an interrupt of the CPU whenever data are ready to be read.
- In a polling system, sensors are periodically checked by the CPU to see if data are ready to be read.

Interrupt-driven systems are modeled with blocking receive statements. To model polling systems, PROMELA supports polling receive statements. Only buffered channels can be polled.

Polling receive statements are not the same as receive statements that do not remove messages from a channel:

```
ch ?? <green, time, false>
```

Although the message is not removed from the channel, copying values into the variables creates a side-effect so the statement cannot be used in a guard. A polling expression (written with square brackets) is *side-effect free* and can be used in a guard:

```
do
:: ch ?? [green, time, false] ->
      ch ?? green, time, false
:: else -> /* Do something else */
od
```

It can also be used in a subexpression of a compound expression, as shown in the following code where we check the channel only on even-numbered executions of the loop body:

```
bool even = true;

   do
   :: even && ch ?? [green, time, false] ->
         ch ?? green, time, false;
         even = !even
   :: else ->
         /* Do something else */
         even = !even
   od
```

Since the evaluation of a guard and the execution of the first statement after the guard are two separate atomic operations, if other processes also receive from the channel, it is possible that the poll statement

```
ch ?? [green, time, false]
```

will be true, but that due to interleaving, the receive statement

```
ch ?? green, time, false
```

will no longer be executable. This can be solved by placing the **do**-statement within **atomic**.

7.9 Comparing rendezvous and buffered channels

The choice between using rendezvous or buffered channels in a model depends on several factors, so the analysis of the tradeoffs between them is a significant aspect of modeling a system.

Rendezvous channels are far more efficient. There is no "variable" associated with a rendezvous channel, so using one does not increase the size of a state. Buffered channels, on the other hand, greatly increase the potential size of the state space because every permutation of messages up to the capacity of the channel might occur in a computation, and the messages themselves can have multiple fields. Furthermore, rendezvous channels are unique in that a single step of a computation causes changes in values of the location counters of more than one process.

In a sense, a buffered channel is just a convenience because it could be implemented with rendezvous channels and an additional process to store the contents of the channel. Programming languages like OCCAM and ADA take precisely this approach and support only communication by rendezvous. However, the convenience of using buffered channels contributes significantly to the ease of constructing models. They facilitate modeling communi-

cations systems that contain channels that can store messages. Buffered channels also enable direct modeling of asynchronous systems where processes
transfer data without blocking.

When a buffered channel is used in a model, the channel capacity must be
carefully considered. A large capacity may be more realistic, but can cause an
explosion in the size of the state space that can make verification impractical.
Section 11.8 gives an example of how to choose the channel capacity to enable
verification.

8

Nondeterminism*

Nondeterminism is a concept that appears in many areas of computer science such as automata theory, algorithms, and concurrency. It is a difficult concept to learn because we intuitively think of computers as carrying out instructions in a step-by-step deterministic fashion. This is apparent when one considers the cliché that compares an algorithm to a cooking recipe; one hardly expects a recipe to include instructions like "chop the onions finely or coarsely" or "heat the oven to 180 or 220 degrees"!

In this chapter we stray somewhat from our introduction to SPIN as a model checker in order to show how SPIN can be used to facilitate learning about nondeterminism. SPIN is an excellent tool for this purpose, both because of the nondeterministic constructs in the PROMELA language and because of the nondeterministic nature of simulations. Furthermore, SPIN itself is based upon the theory of automata, as we discuss in Chapter 10.

First we show how to write a PROMELA program to simulate a *nondeterministic finite automata (NDFA)*; then, we describe VN, a software tool that generates and runs PROMELA programs that model NDFAs. The last section relates $\mathcal{NP}$ problems to simulation and verification in SPIN. This chapter necessarily presumes familiarity with these concepts that are taught as part of the undergraduate curriculum in computer science.

Two additional nondeterministic algorithms are given in the case studies in Section 11.2.

8.1 Nondeterministic finite automata

Figure 8.1 shows an NDFA that accepts the language defined by the regular expression $a^*((bb)^+ + bc^*)$: zero or more occurrences of a followed by either one or more occurrences of bb, or one occurrence of b followed by zero or

Fig. 8.1. NDFA accepting $a^*((bb)^+ + bc^*)$

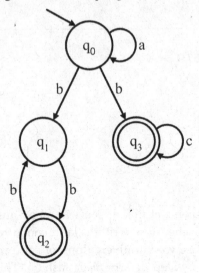

more occurrences of c. The automaton remains in state q_0 as long as there are occurrences of a in the input; when a b is encountered, it nondeterministically chooses to take the transition to q_1 or the transition to q_3. From q_1, the automation can loop between q_1 and q_2 to accept $(bb)^+$; from q_3, it can loop back to q_3 to accept bc^*.

Listing 8.1 shows the translation of the NDFA into PROMELA. The input string "aabb." is given as the initial value of the array i (lines 6–7), and each state is implemented by an **if**-statement whose alternatives are the possible transitions from that state (lines 8–23). A transition is modeled by a **goto**-statement that refers to the label of the **if**-statement representing the target state of the transition. The nondeterminism in state q_0 is readily apparent from the two identical guards that evaluate to true if the input character is 'b' (lines 10–11).

States q_2 and q_3 are final states, so if the end of the input denoted by a period is reached in those states, control transfers to the label accept and a message is printed.[1]

What happens if the input string is rejected? By definition, an input string is rejected if the end of the input has not been reached and there is no transition for the current symbol; in that case, there are no executable alternatives in the **if**-statement and the process blocks. Similarly, an automaton rejects

---

[1] The label accept (line 24) is natural in the context of NDFAs, but it is not a good choice of name in the context of a PROMELA program because of the special meaning it has (see Section 10.3).

Listing 8.1. Nondeterministic finite automaton for $a^*((bb)^+ + bc^*)$

```
1   #define LEN 5
2
3   active proctype FA() {
4     byte h;
5     byte i[LEN];
6     i[0] = 'a'; i[1] = 'a'; i[2] = 'b'; i[3] = 'b';
7     i[4] = '.';
8   q0: if
9     :: i[h] == 'a' -> h++; goto q0
10    :: i[h] == 'b' -> h++; goto q1
11    :: i[h] == 'b' -> h++; goto q3
12    fi;
13  q1: if
14    :: i[h] == 'b' -> h++; goto q2
15    fi;
16  q2: if
17    :: i[h] == 'b' -> h++; goto q1
18    :: i[h] == '.' -> goto accept
19    fi;
20  q3: if
21    :: i[h] == 'c' -> h++; goto q3
22    :: i[h] == '.' -> goto accept
23    fi;
24  accept:
25    printf("Accepted!\n")
26  }
```

a string if it is not in a final state when the end of the input is reached; but the '.' character is read only in final states, so in this case, too, the process blocks. Since there is only one process, the entire computation blocks, and SPIN will terminate with the message timeout.

This PROMELA program was generated automatically by the VN software tool from a file describing the states and transitions of an automaton (see Section 8.2 and Appendix A.4).

8.1.1 `timeout`

In SPIN, occurrences of a timeout state can be detected. The predefined boolean variable **timeout** is true if and only if there are no executable statements in *any* process. It is convenient to look upon **timeout** as similar to a global **else**: While **else** is executable when there are no executable guards in the enclosing **if**- or **do**-statement, **timeout** is executable when there are no executable statements anywhere in the program.

By detecting a timeout, we can arrange to print a message when an input string is rejected. We add an additional process `Watchdog` that contains just one guarded statement:

```
active proctype Watchdog() {
  timeout -> printf("Rejected ...\n")
}
```

The guard – the expression **timeout** – will not become executable until the main process is blocked; then it will become executable and the **printf** statement, which is always executable, will print the message that the input is rejected.

The expression **timeout** is discussed further in Section 4.7 on the termination of processes, and in Section 11.3 where it is used to model discrete time.

8.1.2 Using verification to find accepting computations

Random simulation is not a good way of investigating NDFAs. An NDFA accepts an input string if *there exists* a computation that terminates in a final state, so it may be necessary to run a simulation dozens of times to get an accepting computation, and if one is not obtained it does not mean that one does not exist.

In verification mode SPIN performs a search over all possible ways of resolving nondeterminism. To check if an NDFA accepts an input string, verify the program with **assert(false)** placed at the end of the process FA. If there exists an accepting computation of the NDFA, then there exists a computation of the PROMELA program in which the process terminates. SPIN will find this computation as a counterexample to the claim that **false** is true, and from the trail the computation can be reconstructed. If there really are no accepting computations of the NDFA, there are no computations in which the program terminates, and SPIN will report that no errors have been be detected during the verification.

The verifier must be run with the −E argument as described in Section 4.7.2. If a timeout occurs, the `Watchdog` process will print `Rejected` and then terminate, but the process FA remains blocked and does not terminate; this is an invalid end state that is not a counterexample that we want from the verifier.

8.1.3 Finding all counterexamples

Suppose that we want to find all inputs of length four that lead to accepting computations in the NDFA of Figure 8.1. This is easy enough to arrange by selecting the elements of the input string nondeterministically:

```
inline Input(n) {
  if
  :: i[n] = 'a'
  :: i[n] = 'b'
  :: i[n] = 'c'
  fi
}

active proctype FA() {
  byte h;
  byte i[LEN];
  Input(0); Input(1); Input(2); Input(3);
  i[4] = '.';
  . . .
}
```

SPIN is optimized for finding the *first* counterexample, but it is possible to request that it find all of them. Run the verifier with the following arguments:

```
pan -E -c0 -e
```

The argument -c0 requests the verifier to keep searching even if errors have been found, and the argument -e requests the verifier to write trail files for all errors. For the modified program (in file fa1.pml), we find that there are six counterexamples; the trail files will be named fa1.pmlN.trail, where N goes from 1 to 6. To run a guided simulation with a specific trail file, add its number to the -t argument:

```
spin -t4 fa1.pml
```

By examining the output, we can determine that the six inputs of length four that have accepting computations are:

```
aaab, aabb, aabc, abcc, bbbb, bccc
```

Fig. 8.2. NDFA with λ transitions accepting $a^*((bb)^+ + bc^*)$

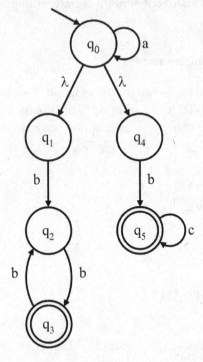

8.1.4 λ-transitions

An alternate NDFA for $a^*((bb)^+ + bc^*)$ is shown in Figure 8.2. It is the NDFA that would be obtained by separately constructing NDFAs for $(bb)^+$ and bc^*, and then concatenating them with the trivial automaton for a^*. This NDFA has λ-transitions,[2] which are transitions that can be taken without reading a character from the input. In this NDFA the λ-transitions are used to nondeterministically choose whether to continue looking for a's or to start looking for the first b. We leave it to the reader to write a PROMELA program for this NDFA.

---

[2] These are also called ϵ-transitions.

Fig. 8.3. Rejecting path in VN

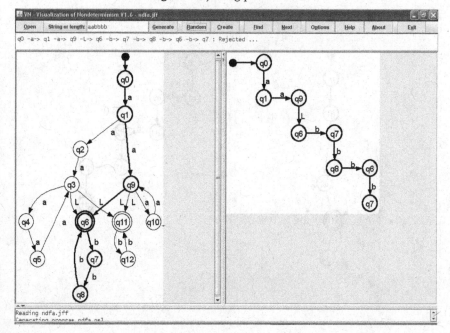

8.2 VN: Visualizing nondeterminism

VN is a software tool for visualizing the nondeterminism of an NDFA. Figures 8.3–8.4 show screenshots of VN with the state diagram for an NDFA displayed in the left pane.[3] The NDFA in the figures is for the language $a^m b^n$, such that $m \geq 2$, $n \geq 0$, and both m and n are divisible by two or three.[4]

The design of VN is described in Appendix A.4. The NDFA is read from a file in the format that is written by JFLAP [18], which is an interactive software tool for studying formal languages and automata. An input string, such as *aabbbb*, is entered in the text field on the toolbar and Generate selected. This causes a PROMELA program similar to the one in Listing 8.1 to be generated. The program can now be run in several modes based upon the modes of SPIN:

Random – SPIN executes the program in random simulation mode. A single computation is created by randomly resolving the nondeterminacy.
Create – SPIN executes the program in interactive simulation mode, so that you can interactively resolve each nondeterministic choice.

---

[3] The λ-transitions are denoted by the letter L.
[4] This NDFA is example 1.3 from [18].

Fig. 8.4. An accepting path in VN

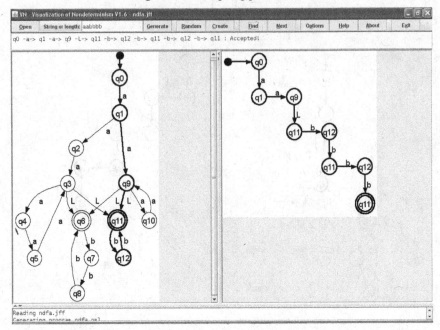

Find – The assertion **assert(false)** is added to the end of the generated
program and a verification is performed. If a counterexample is found,
it indicates that an accepting computation of the NDFA exists. A guided
simulation run with the trail creates this computation.

Next – The verifier is run again to search for the next counterexample, if any.

Figure 8.3 shows a rejecting computation obtained by a random simulation,
while Figure 8.4 shows an accepting computation obtained by verification.

An accepting or rejecting computation is displayed in three ways:

- The list of the states and the input symbols that caused each transition is
  displayed in a text field beneath the toolbar.
- The path is displayed in the right pane.
- States and transitions in the path are emphasized in the diagram of the
  NDFA in the left pane.

The list in the text field and the path in the right pane display the entire
computation which may visit the same state many times. In the left pane a
state or transition is emphasized only once; the purpose of this display is to
enable you to trace the computation through the NDFA.

By entering a number instead of an input string in the text field in the toolbar, Find and Next will display *all* accepting computations for *all* input strings whose length is less than or equal to the value entered in the field.

Experiment with input strings of various lengths to get a feel for how often a random simulation of the NDFA leads to an accepting computation for an input string. Compare this with the time its takes for a SPIN verification performed during Find to carry out an exhaustive search in order to find an accepting computation. For example, I performed one hundred random simulations for the input string $a^9 b^8$ and they were all rejecting, but an accepting computation was obtained within a couple of seconds by selecting Find.

8.3 $\mathcal{NP}$ problems

An algorithmic problem is in the class $\mathcal{P}$ if it can be solved by a *deterministic* algorithm in *polynomial* time; that is, its running time is a polynomial function of the length of the input. A problem is in the class $\mathcal{NP}$ if it can be solved by a *nondeterministic* algorithm in *polynomial* time. The definition of nondeterminism here is similar to that of NDFAs: a nondeterministic algorithm solves a problem if, given any input, *there exists* a computation that produces the correct answer.

Consider a formula in the propositional calculus such as

$$A = (a \vee c) \wedge (\neg a \vee \neg c) \wedge (a \vee \neg b) \wedge (\neg a \vee b) \wedge (b \vee \neg c) \wedge (\neg b \vee \neg c).$$

Let v be an assignment of truth values to the atomic formulas of A:

$$v(a) = T, \; v(b) = T, \; v(c) = F.$$

It is trivial to check that the truth value of A is in fact true under the assignment v simply by substituting the values from v into A and computing the truth value of A using the truth tables for the propositional operators $\vee$ and $\wedge$. Thus, there is an efficient algorithm for solving the following problem: Given an arbitrary formula A of the propositional calculus *and* an arbitrary assignment v, is A true under v? The algorithm runs in time that is polynomial in lengths of A and v, so the problem is in the class $\mathcal{P}$.

Consider now a different problem: Given an arbitrary formula of the propositional calculus A, is A *satisfiable*, that is, does there *exist* an assignment v that makes A true? This problem is called the *satisfiability problem for the propositional calculus (SAT)*. It is easy to see that *SAT* is in $\mathcal{NP}$: Generate an assignment nondeterministically and then check if it satisfies the formula. Clearly, generating an assignment v takes very little time, and we have shown that checking the truth of A under a given assignment is also efficient. If a formula is satisfiable, *there exists* a computation that returns the answer true, and if not, no computation returns true. We conclude that there is a polynomial-time nondeterministic algorithm for *SAT*, thus the problem is in the class $\mathcal{NP}$.

The PROMELA program in Listing 8.2 uses a nondeterministic **if**-statement to generate an assignment and then computes the truth value of the formula A given above. By running half a dozen random simulations of this program, the above assignment v for which A is true was obtained.

Listing 8.2. Satisfiability in the propositional calculus

```
1   active proctype P() {
2     bool a, b, c, result;
3
4     if :: a = true :: a = false fi;
5     if :: b = true :: b = false fi;
6     if :: c = true :: c = false fi;
7
8     result =
9       (a || c) && (!a || !c) &&
10      (a || !b) && (!a || b) &&
11      (b || !c) && (!b || !c);
12
13    printf("a = %d, b = %d, c = %d, result = %d\n",
14          a, b, c, result)
15  }
```

A slight modification of the formula A (removing the final $\neg$) gives the formula A':

$$A' = (a \vee c) \wedge (\neg a \vee \neg c) \wedge (a \vee \neg b) \wedge (\neg a \vee b) \wedge (b \vee \neg c) \wedge (\neg b \vee c)$$

that is *unsatisfiable*, that is, A' is a formula whose truth value is false under *all* assignments. No matter how many random simulations we run, we will never get that result is true, but we can never be sure that *all* possible assignments have been tried.

Only verification can give us the definitive answer that A' is unsatisfiable by checking its truth value under all assignments. In the program in Listing 8.2, remove the negation on the second occurrence of c in line 11 and add the statement

assert (!result)

at the end of the program. Running SPIN in verification mode reports that there are *no* errors, meaning that regardless of the choices made in the nondeterministic statement (lines 4–6), the expression !result is always *true*. We conclude that the formula is unsatisfiable.

Add **assert** (!result) to the program with the satisfiable formula *A* and run a verification. Now, there will be choices for the values of the variables a, b, c for which the value of the variable result is true. This falsifies the expression !result, so SPIN will report an error and a guided simulation with the trail will produce the assignment.

Verification is a purely deterministic algorithm because SPIN systematically generates and checks all possible states for errors. The verification algorithm in SPIN demonstrates that *any nondeterministic algorithm can be mechanically transformed into a deterministic one*: instead of choosing nondeterministically among several alternatives, execute the algorithm for *all* possible choices. Unfortunately, this is highly inefficient. It is easy to see that given n variables, there are 2^n different sets of choices for assigning truth values to them, and all of these must be checked. If the formula happens to be unsatisfiable, the algorithm does not terminate until it has checked all possible assignments.

The software archive accompanying this book contains PROMELA programs for checking the satisfiability of formulas with a large number of variables. Try running simulations and verifications on them and experience the difference in running time. You will find that random simulations run very quickly even for a program with a large number of variables, but as the number of variables increases much above 20, verification becomes impracticable. Methods for optimizing verification runs are discussed in Section 10.2.

Is *SAT* in $\mathcal{P}$? That is a million-dollar question. Literally! The question $\mathcal{P} = \mathcal{NP}$? – is there a deterministic polynomial algorithm for any problem solvable by a nondeterministic polynomial algorithm – is so difficult and so fundamental that it is on the list of the *Millennium Problems* compiled by the Clay Mathematics Institute which offers a prize of one million dollars for the solution of any of the problems.[5]

The difference between random simulation and verification brings to life the concept of a problem in $\mathcal{NP}$. Simulation efficiently "guesses" an answer nondeterministically and then checks if it is correct, while verification can

---

[5] claymath.org.

find an answer deterministically if one exists. SPIN performs verification using a relatively inefficient exhaustive search, but no one knows if there is a deterministic algorithm that is significantly more efficient than the exhaustive search.

Advanced: Generation of the unsatisfiable formulas

The unsatisfiable formulas were automatically generated from graphs according to a procedure developed by G.C.Tseitin (see Section 4.4 of *MLCS*). In the archive are PROMELA programs corresponding to the complete bipartite graphs $K_{3,3}$, $K_{4,4}$, and $K_{5,5}$ with 9, 16, and 25 variables, respectively. For the first two programs both simulation and verification run very fast. For the third program the computation in simulation mode terminates immediately, but verification is beyond the capability of my computer. For the experiments described in Section 10.2, I used a version of the third program with only 23 variables that was obtained by removing the literals corresponding to two edges of $K_{5,5}$.

9

Advanced Topics in PROMELA*

This chapter surveys constructs of PROMELA that are used less often than the ones that have been discussed. The intent is to bring them to the attention of the reader, rather than to explain their use in detail. For more information see *SMC* and the *man* pages.

9.1 Specifiers for variables

Certain specifiers can be applied to the declarations of variables. They must be used with care since they affect the way that variables are treated during verification.

hidden If a global variable is specified as **hidden**, its value will not be part of the states of the computation. It is an alternative to the use of the anonymous variable _ described below.

local Specifying that a global variables is **local** indicates to SPIN that the variable is accessed by only one process. The only reason you would declare a variable used by one process to be global is to enable it to be used in a never claim (Section 10.3); adding the **local** specifier can then enable optimization.

xr, xs These specifiers can be applied to a channel variable and specify that a process has exclusive receive (**xr**) or exclusive send (**xs**) access to the channel. This information is then used to optimize verification. The specifiers cannot be used within a process *type* that is instantiated more than once because that would violate the exclusivity, nor can they be used for rendezvous channels.

show The specifier **show** is used with the XSPIN environment (*SMC*, Chapter 12).

9.2 Predefined variables

PROMELA has several predefined variables, some of which we have encountered before. Predefined variables and functions that are intended for use only in never claims are described in Section 10.3.4.

9.2.1 The anonymous variable

There is a single predefined global anonymous variable written as an underscore _. The variable replaces "dummy" variables used in other languages, and has the advantage that its value is not part of the states of a computation, so no memory is required to store it during a verification. The most common use is in receive statements, where the values of some or all of the message fields are not needed (see Listing 7.3).

Another example of the use of the anonymous variable is shown in the PROMELA solution for the *dining philosophers problem* taken from Sections 8.4–8.5 of *PCDP* and shown in Listing 9.1. Both the philosophers and the forks are modeled by processes that communicate over channels. There is one channel for each fork. A process Phil waits to receive messages from two forks (lines 6–7) and replies on the *same channels* when it has finished eating (lines 9–10). In a process Fork, if the fork is in use the process is blocked on its receive statement (line 17); this ensures mutual exclusion. The channels are used just for synchronization and not to pass data; since the messages have no content and are always true, anonymous variables can be used.

This solution is not correct because it can deadlock.

9.2.2 Process identifiers

The predefined variable **_pid** is read-only and local to each process; it gives a unique number to each process as it is instantiated. The variable is of type **pid** and takes values from 0 to 254 (not 255). Section 3.5 showed how to use **_pid** to identify processes that are created by **active proctype** and so cannot be initialized from parameters.

The predefined variable **_nr_pr** is read-only and global; its value is the number of active processes. In Section 3.5 we used the expression

    (_nr_pr == 1)

in the **init** process to wait for the termination of all other processes.

Listing 9.1. Solution of the dining philosophers problem

```
1   chan forks[5] = [0] of { bool };
2
3   proctype Phil(byte n; chan left; chan right ) {
4     do
5     :: printf("Philosopher %d is thinking\n", n);
6        left ? _;
7        right ? _;
8        printf("Philosopher %d is eating\n", n);
9        right ! true;
10       left ! true
11    od
12  }
13
14  proctype Fork(chan ch) {
15    do
16    :: ch ! true;
17       ch ? _
18    od
19  }
20
21  init {
22    atomic {
23      run Fork(forks[0]);
24      run Fork(forks[1]);
25      run Fork(forks[2]);
26      run Fork(forks[3]);
27      run Fork(forks[4]);
28      run Phil(0,forks[0],forks[1]);
29      run Phil(1,forks[1],forks[2]);
30      run Phil(2,forks[2],forks[3]);
31      run Phil(3,forks[3],forks[4]);
32      run Phil(4,forks[4],forks[0]);
33    }
34  }
```

9.3 Priority

9.3.1 Simulation priority

A **priority** for a process can be specified either on an **active proctype** declaration or on a **run** statement that instantiates a process type declared by **proctype**:

```
active proctype Important( ... ) priority 10 {
    ...
}

proctype NotImportant( ... ) {
    ...
}

run NotImportant( ... ) priority 2;
```

However, this priority is not the same as the familiar hierarchal priorities of operating systems, where a process will *not* be executed if a process with a higher priority is ready. In SPIN priority is meaningful only in random simulation mode; the specification **priority** 10 for a process simply means that this process is ten times more likely than a process with default priority 1 to be chosen for execution.

9.3.2 Modeling priority with global constraints

It is possible to model simple hierarchal priority schemes in PROMELA using **provided**. This specification is attached to a **proctype** declaration and includes the keyword **provided** followed by an expression; the expression becomes an additional guard on *all* the statements of the process:

```
bool ok;

proctype P( ... ) provided (ok) {
    ...
}
```

If another process sets the variable ok to false at any time, process P will no longer be selected for execution during a simulation, and states obtained by executing a statement from P will no longer be searched during a verification. Only when a process resets ok to true, will statements from P become executable.

Listing 9.2. Modeling an interrupt handler with **provided**

```
1   byte n = 0;
2   bool interrupt = false;
3
4   proctype Compute() provided (!interrupt) {
5     n = n + 1
6   }
7
8   proctype Interrupt() {
9     byte temp;
10    interrupt = true;
11    temp = n + 1;
12    n = temp;
13    interrupt = false
14  }
15
16  init {
17    atomic {
18      run Interrupt();
19      run Compute()
20    }
21    (_nr_pr == 1);
22    assert (n == 2)
23  }
```

An interesting example of the use of **provided** is in a model that demonstrates *priority inversion*, which is an unexpected behavior in priority-driven systems that actually occurred in the computer system of the Mars Pathfinder spacecraft. The model also demonstrates *priority inheritance*, which is a mechanism for avoiding priority inversion. This example is discussed in depth in *SMC*, Chapter 5, and in *PCDP*, Sections 13.7 and 13.8.

Listing 9.2 shows a simple model of an interrupt handler which is to have a higher priority than "ordinary" computation. The program is composed of a process Compute that models the ordinary computation, and a process Interrupt that models the interrupt handler. The handler sets a flag interrupt upon entry (line 10) and resets it upon exit (line 13). The **provided** specification (line 4) ensures that the increment instruction in process Compute cannot be executed while the interrupt handler is executing;

Listing 9.3. Handling division by zero

```
1   active proctype Divide() {
2     int n = 1;
3   end:
4     do
5     :: {
6           ch ? n;
7           printf("%d\n", 100 / n)
8         } unless {
9           n == 0 ->
10              printf("Attempt to divide by zero\n")
11        }
12     od
13  }
```

therefore, the instruction n = n + 1 in line 5 cannot have its execution in-
terleaved between the instructions temp = n + 1 and n = temp on lines 11
and 12.

First, run a verification without the **provided** specifier. SPIN will report
an error: the violation of the assertion in line 22, which was caused by the
interleaving described above. Replace the **provided** specifier and the error
disappears because the specifier prevents the interleaving.

The use of **provided** should be avoided, if possible, because SPIN cannot
perform the partial order reduction optimization when it is used.

9.4 Modeling exceptions

Exceptions are unexpected runtime states. Modern programming languages
have a construct such as try-catch to enable an exception handler to be associated with a sequence of statements so that the occurrence of an exception
within the sequence can be caught and handled. In PROMELA an **unless**-
block can be associated with a statement or sequence of statements and is executed only if its guard (the first statement in the block) becomes executable.

Listing 9.3 shows a process that receives a sequence of **int** values from a
channel (line 6) and uses each value as a divisor (line 7); an **unless**-block is
used to avoid division by zero: Before each statement in the block is executed,
the guard of the **unless** is checked (line 9). If a zero value is received, the

guard n == 0 becomes true and the error message is printed instead of the division being executed.

In many cases, the same effect can be obtained more simply by using an **if**-statement:

```
ch ? n;
if
:: n == 0 ->
    printf("Attempt to divide by zero\n")
:: else ->
    printf("%d\n", 100 / n)
fi
```

The **unless** construct should be reserved for situations where an event can occur at arbitrary points within the computation. See Figure 3.1 of *SMC* for an example: in a model of a telephone exchange, the system must always be able to handle the event that occurs when a subscriber hangs up, and this can occur at any time during a call.

9.5 Reading from standard input

There is a predefined read-only channel called STDIN which is connected to standard input. It can be useful in controlling simulations interactively, or to run a sequence of simulations parameterized by data from a file as an alternative to using conditional compilation (Section 6.3.1):

```
byte version;
STDIN ? version;
currentPriority = (
  (version == 1) ? (p1 > p2 -> p1 : p2) :
  (version == 2) ? PMAX :
                   PMIN );
```

9.6 Embedded C code

PROMELA is designed as a language for modeling systems that are to be verified by SPIN; it is very limited in its expressiveness in order that verification be efficient. Once a model has been verified, it must then be translated into a program in an ordinary programming language for execution on a real system; in addition, parts of the system that were not modeled must be implemented. There is a real possibility that the transition from model to program can introduce errors. An active field of research is to try to extend model checking techniques to real programs.

As a step in that direction, SPIN can simulate and verify PROMELA models with embedded C code. The intention is that algorithms written in C can form part of the model, even if SPIN cannot prove the algorithms themselves. For example, a flight control system could incorporate algorithms requiring floating-point computation. Even though these computations cannot be written in PROMELA nor can they be verified with SPIN, it does make sense to verify properties of the control system, such as absence of deadlock. Furthermore, since the inputs to the algorithms are usually discrete samples from sensors, as are the commands to the actuators, the input-output relation can be modeled in PROMELA. This implies that the model can be verified in SPIN *under the assumption* that the embedded floating-point computation is correct.

Embedded C code is fully explained in Chapter 17 of *SMC*.

Advanced Topics in SPIN*

The success of SPIN in industrial software development is primarily due to the efficiency with which it carries out verifications. The efficiency results in part from the architecture of SPIN (Figure 2.1), which generates a verifier that is optimized for a particular model, correctness specification, and search method. The verifier is written in C, a relatively low-level language that can be optimized by compilers. Nevertheless, even the most efficient verifier will run up against limitations of time and memory, so that the task of the systems engineer is to find the appropriate tradeoffs between model complexity and resources. SPIN supports various ways of optimizing the use of resources, in particular, memory.

To profit from these options you must have a basic understanding of how SPIN verifies models written in PROMELA; we give an overview of this topic in Section 10.1. Section 10.2 surveys techniques for optimizing verifications in SPIN. Section 10.3 describes how correctness specifications in temporal logic are translated into never claims in PROMELA, and Section 10.4 presents non-progress cycles, an alternate technique for verifying liveness properties.

If you intend to use any of the constructs introduced in this chapter, you should read their full description in *SMC* or the *man* pages.

A prerequisite for understanding the material in this chapter is a basic familiarity with data structures such as directed graphs and hash tables.

10.1 How SPIN searches the state space

Consider again the state transition diagram in Figure 4.1. The diagram is repeated here in a somewhat reduced format:

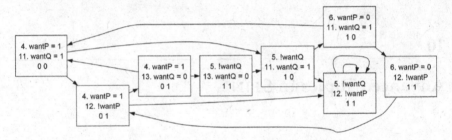

We already know that this solution to the critical section problem is incorrect because of the deadlock. How can SPIN discover that this error state exists? Clearly, it must search the state space represented by the graph, starting from the initial state $(4,11)$.[1]

Let us follow a systematic *depth-first search* from the initial node. We also assume that the transitions in a state are ordered with those resulting from the execution of a statement from process P coming first. The initial steps of the search give us the path:

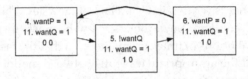

As shown by the bold arrow, the third step would be to return to the initial state, but this state is not a *new* state that needs to be searched. The set of nodes that have been visited on a path in a depth-first search is stored in a stack, so by checking the stack it is possible to determine that the state has already been visited and need not be searched again. Therefore, the search backtracks and tries the transition from state $(6,11)$ associated with the second process; this leads to $(6,12)$. Continuing again with the transitions for the first process, the search quickly leads to state $(5,12)$ and there are no transitions out of the state:

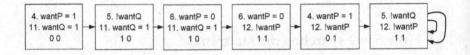

---

[1] The values of the variables will be omitted from the states in the discussion in this section because each state is unambiguously identified by the control points of the two processes.

SPIN reports the invalid end state and terminates the search.

The advantage of the depth-first search is that a stack suffices to maintain the history of the search; the only data you need to store is the sequence of the states on the path to the current state, together with an indication for each state which transition was the last one taken. In the worst case, of course, the entire state diagram might be a linear sequence of states, but more commonly, the state diagram will be highly connected so that the size of the paths will be significantly less than the total number of states.

Suppose now that we are not interested in the deadlock state, but rather in verifying if mutual exclusion holds. Assume that the method described in Section 5.7 is used – specifying mutual exclusion using remote references – so that no new variables and states are needed. Furthermore, assume that pan is run with the -E argument so that the verifier does not stop at invalid end states like the deadlocked state. The depth-first search by the verifier begins as before, but now it backtracks from the deadlocked state (5,12). Eventually, SPIN will generate the following computation, where from state (5,11) the transition leads to state (6,11):

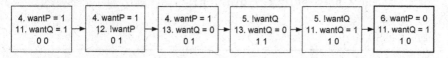

Although the state does not appear on the stack, there is no point in continuing the search from this state, because it appeared earlier in the search (see the third state from the left in the last diagram on the previous page). Unfortunately, the state is no longer on the stack, but for an efficient search it is important to maintain a data structure that stores *all* states that have been visited. During verification SPIN expends most of its resources (time and memory) storing states in this data structure and looking up newly created states to see if they have been visited before. The next section describes the various methods that SPIN uses to maintain the data structure and the tradeoffs involved in choosing a method.

SPIN does not actually "search the graph" in the sense that the graph is constructed and then searched; instead, for each transition that is considered, SPIN builds the target state "on-the-fly." This can make the search much more efficient because SPIN need only construct states until the first counterexample is found. Of course, if there are no errors, all the states in the state space will eventually be built, so the on-the-fly construction saves nothing, but in most cases it is efficient because we construct more models with errors than we do error-free models!

Listing 10.1. Generating input in a separate process

```
1   #include "for.h"
2   chan ch = [0] of { byte };
3
4   active proctype Producer() {
5     for (i, 1, 10)
6       if
7       :: ch ! 0
8       :: ch ! 10
9       :: ch ! 20
10      fi
11    rof (i)
12  }
13
14  active proctype Consumer() {
15    byte n;
16  end:
17    do
18    :: ch ? n -> printf("%d\n", n)
19    od
20  }
```

10.2 Optimizing the performance of verifications

10.2.1 Writing efficient models

The performance of SPIN depends critically on how efficiently it can update and search a data structure that stores the states that have been visited. The data stored for each state, called the *state vector*, consist of the location counters of the processes and the values of the variables, for example, (4,11,0,0). Clearly, verification will be more efficient if the amount of memory needed to store a state vector is as small as possible; there are several things you can do to reduce this:

- Use as few processes as possible. For example, if a process serves only to generate data to be sent on a channel, you can remove the process and generate the data *within* the process receiving the data using a non-deterministic statement to select the message "received." Consider the program in Listing 10.1. We can remove the channel ch and the first

Listing 10.2. Generating input in the same process

```
1  #include "for.h"
2  active proctype Consumer() {
3    byte n;
4    for (i, 1, 10)
5      if
6      :: n = 0
7      :: n = 10
8      :: n = 20
9      fi;
10     printf("%d\n", n)
11   rof (i)
12 }
```

process by moving the nondeterministic generation of data into the second process (Listing 10.2). This reduces the size of the state vector from 20 bytes to 12 bytes and the number of distinct states from 123 to 64. Another example of this technique is given in Section 11.8.

- Do not declare unnecessary variables, and declare variables with as narrow a type as possible; so, **byte** is preferable to **int**, and **bit** or **bool** is preferable to **byte**.
- Avoid declaring channel capacities in excess of what is needed to verify the model.
- Use **atomic** and **d_step** where possible, but be sure that you are not "masking" possible error states by incorrectly restricting the interleaving.

Memory requirements will *not* be reduced in the following cases:

- A value of an **mtype** is stored in a full byte, regardless of the number of symbols defined.
- An array whose elements are of type **bit** or **bool** is stored as an array of type **byte**. Section 11.7.2 shows how to encode sets of bits into bytes.

For detailed information on memory management see Chapter 9 of *SMC*.

10.2.2 Allocating memory for the hash table

SPIN uses a hash table to store the state vectors that have been previously encountered. A hash function computes an index from the state vector considered as an uninterpreted sequence of bytes, and this index is used to access an element of a large array where (pointers to) the state vectors are stored. Since the hash function can map different state vectors into the same index, it can happen that the element of the hash array is already occupied; this is called a *hash conflict*. In case of a hash conflict, the element of the array is used as the head of a linked list where all state vectors that map to this index are stored. It is important to reduce the number of hash conflicts because the linear search of a list is inefficient.

The following diagram shows a schematic representation of the hash table of state vectors:

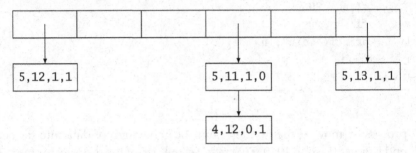

The implications of this data structure are as follows:

- The smaller the state vector, the larger the number of elements in the hash table for a given amount of memory.
- The larger the number of elements in the hash table, the more likely it becomes that state vectors can be stored directly in the table without a hash conflict.

During a long verification, the verifier prints out progress reports after every million states have been searched. Here is part of the list of reports for the 23-variable version of the program in Listing 8.2:

```
Depth=24 States=1e+006 Transitions=1.49999e+006 Memory=17.548
Depth=24 States=2e+006 Transitions=2.99999e+006 Memory=33.522
```

⋮

```
Depth=24 States=1.5e+007 Transitions=2.25e+007 Memory=241.497
Depth=24 States=1.6e+007 Transitions=2.4e+007 Memory=257.573
```

The information includes the depth reached in the depth-first search, the number of states and transitions searched, and the amount of memory used in megabytes. At the very least, these messages give some reassurance that the verifier is actually making some progress! You can always terminate the execution if the verification is taking too long or running out of memory (Section 5.3.3).

At the end of a verification, the verifier prints data on the use of memory:

```
State-vector 16 byte, depth reached 24, errors: 0
1.67772e+007 states, stored
8.38861e+006 states, matched
2.51658e+007 transitions (= stored+matched)
hash conflicts: 6.58266e+008 (resolved)
269.964 total actual memory usage
```

The first line shows that the size of the state vector is 16 bytes, which is actually quite small, but this is to be expected because the variables are of type **bool** and can be compressed. The search depth is also shown; this is as expected because the verification must assign values to 23 variables and then compute the expression in **result**.

The next lines are the most important because they report on the efficiency of the hash table. About 16.8 million state vectors were stored in the hash table, while another 8.4 million were found to be in the table when they were generated by the search. We see that the check for previously generated states reduced the number of state vectors that need be stored by one third.

Unfortunately, the number of hash conflicts was 658 million, and this indicates that most of the execution time went into searching the linked lists associated with conflicting hash table entries. Clearly, it is worthwhile increasing the number of elements in the table. The size of the state vector is so small that it cannot be further compressed, but since we used only 270 megabytes of memory (as printed in the last line of the verification report above), it is possible to allocate more memory to the hash table. The default for the number entries in the table is $2^{18} = 256K$, and it can be increased using the -w argument when executing the verifier:

```
pan -w20
```

The following table shows how increasing the size of the hash table increases the amount of memory needed by a moderate amount while greatly reducing the number of hash conflicts and thus the running time of the verification:

Hash table (2^w)	Memory (MB)	Conflicts ($\times 10^6$)	Time (sec)
18	270	658	86
20	273	151	33
22	286	52	22
24	336	29	18
26	537	0.1	17

An initial modest increase in the size of the hash table to $2^{20} = 1M$ elements dramatically improves the performance of the verifier from 86 to 33 seconds, but a larger size has only a marginal effect, because the execution time then depends more on factors other than hash conflicts.

Warning

Be alert for *thrashing*. This occurs when the verifier runs out of physical memory so that subsequent allocations cause virtual memory to be used. The excessive I/O to the disk will seriously degrade the performance of the verifier. To prevent thrashing, compile the verifier with the argument -DMEMLIM=n specifying the maximum amount of memory in megabytes that may be allocated.

Advanced: Hashing methods

SPIN implements two additional, extremely efficient, methods for storing the hash table: *bitstate hashing* and *hash compact*. These methods are *lossy* because they may not store all the states that have been visited, so some parts of the state diagram may not be searched and some counterexamples may not found. That is, a *false positive* is possible where no errors are reported although some may exist. Nevertheless, these methods are useful because they do not give *false negatives*, that is, if a counterexample is found, it represents a true error.

10.2.3 Compressing the state vector

The example in the previous section is atypical because the state vector was very small; sizes of several hundred bytes are more common. SPIN implements a sophisticated method for encoding the state vector called *collapse compression*, which is invoked by compiling the verifier with an argument:

```
gcc -DCOLLAPSE (other arguments) -o pan pan.c
```

For example, a verification of a PROMELA program for the Byzantine General's algorithm (Section 12.4 of *PCDP*) had a state vector of 164 bytes that required 127 bytes under the default compression. Using collapse compression, this was reduced to 39 bytes! The memory requirements were reduced accordingly from 66 to 23 megabytes. There is a tradeoff between memory use and execution time because of the time required to compress the state vectors; here, execution time for the verification rose from 6 to 8 seconds.

10.2.4 Minimal automaton

State vectors can be stored without a hash table using a representation called a *minimal automaton* that is similar to the *binary decision diagrams* used in other model checkers [8]. This is invoked with a compile-time argument that gives the size of the automaton:

```
gcc -DMA=10 (other arguments) -o pan pan.c
```

The memory requirements can be reduced to a very small amount, but the execution time is likely to rise significantly. For the program in Listing 8.2 the verification was accomplished using only 0.38 MB, but the execution time increased to 181 seconds. When verifying a larger version of the program, my computer ran out of memory when I tried to use a hash table, but using the minimal automaton the verification was completed using only half a megabyte of memory, although the verification ran for almost 10 minutes.

10.2.5 Partial-order reduction

One of the most important optimizations performed by SPIN is called *partial order reduction*. This avoids creating states that cannot be affected by interleaving the execution for the processes. For example, a multitasking system run on a CPU with registers could be modeled by using global variables for the memory and local variables for the registers:

```
register = n;
register++;
n = register;
```

SPIN can detect that interleaving statements of other processes before or after the increment of the local variable cannot affect any correctness specification because they must use global variables. The manual optimization that we demonstrated in Section 3.4 – combining the increment with one of the other statements – is not strictly necessary, because a similar optimization is achieved by partial order reduction. This optimization is performed by default so you do not need to invoke it. However, a few constructs in PROMELA are not compatible with partial order reduction and should be avoided if possible; these are **_last**, **provided**, **enabled** and remote variable references.

10.3 Never claims

Section 10.1 described how SPIN searches the state transition diagram looking for error states where an assertion evaluates to false or for invalid end

Fig. 10.1. A finitely presented infinite falsifying computation

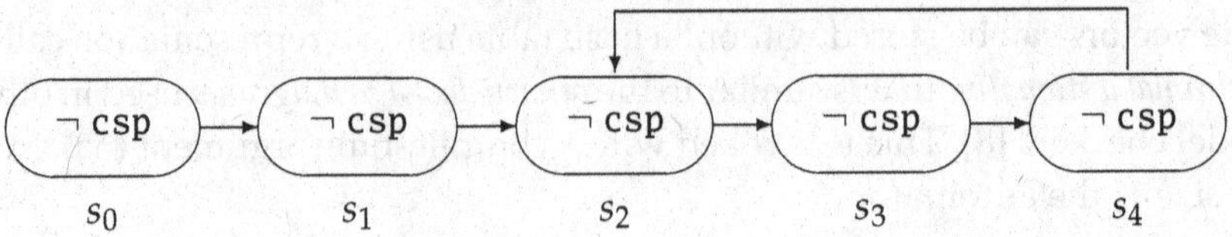

states that can indicate deadlock. Checking correctness properties expressed as formulas of temporal logic is more difficult.

Consider a correctness specification in temporal logic such as <>csp where csp is true if process P is in its critical section (Section 5.4.1). The truth of the formula cannot be evaluated just by looking at a single state; rather, it is true in a state s_0 if there is an accessible state s_k in which csp is true. Therefore, it can be falsified in s_0 only if there exists an infinite computation starting in s_0 in which csp is never true. Since models in PROMELA are finite, an infinite computation must be *finitely presented*, that is, composed of a finite number of distinct states (Figure 10.1). It can be shown that for any correctness specification in temporal logic, *if* there exists an infinite computation in which the specification holds, *then* there exists a finitely presented computation of the form shown in the figure: a finite sequence of states followed by a finite set of states that compose a *strongly connected component* within the state transition diagram.

In Chapter 5 we showed how to specify correctness properties using temporal logic. SPIN transforms a formula in temporal logic into a PROMELA construct called a *never claim*. Just as a PROMELA program specifies an automaton whose state space is searched by the verifier, so a never claim specifies an automaton whose state space is searched in parallel with the one that is defined by the PROMELA program.

SPIN's algorithm for verification is fully described in Chapter 8 of *SMC*; here we outline the place of never claims in the algorithm. We will limit our discussion to never claims obtained by translating a formula in temporal logic, but never claims are constructs in the PROMELA language and can be written directly. There are specifications that can be written as never claims that cannot be written in temporal logic; furthermore, the translation might not generate the most efficient claim. See Chapter 6 of *SMC*. An alternate method of specifying correctness properties is to use a graphic formalism called *timelines* as described in Chapter 13 of *SMC*. Liveness properties can also be verified using non-progress cycles as explained in Section 10.4.

10.3.1 A never claim for a safety property

Let us first consider a specification of a safety property in temporal logic (Section 5.3.3). In an algorithm for solving the critical section problem, define the variable `critical` as usual, together with the symbol:

#define mutex (critical <= 1)

and the specification of safety:

[]mutex

To understand how never claims work, look upon a verification as a competition between you and the verifier generated by SPIN. You claim []mutex, while SPIN aims to show that you are wrong because ![]mutex holds. Although the terminology may seem somewhat cumbersome, this can be expressed as follows: you "win" if it is *never* true that ![]mutex holds, while SPIN "wins" if it can find a computation in which ![]mutex holds. The negation of the correctness specification []mutex is translated into the following never claim:

```
never { /* !([]mutex) */
T0_init:
    if
    :: (! ((mutex))) -> goto accept_all
    :: (1) -> goto T0_init
    fi;
accept_all:
    skip
}
```

The never claim looks similar to an ordinary PROMELA program except that it is composed of expressions and control statements only.

Let the game begin! Like many games, it is conducted by alternating "turns" to move. We will follow the steps of the game first for the case where the correctness claim of mutual exclusion does *not* hold, and then for the case where it does.

After the PROMELA program is initialized, the first turn belongs to SPIN because it is possible that there is a counterexample in the initial state. In the initial state of an algorithm for the critical section problem, mutex is always true because these algorithms always start with all processes in their noncritical sections. The first statement of the never claim is the **if**-statement and, since by assumption mutex is true, !mutex is false, so the only executable alternative is the one guarded by (1).[2] The result of the execution of this

---

[2] Recall that the expression (1) is the same as the expression **true**.

statement is that control returns to the start of the **if**-statement at the label
T0_init.

Now you and SPIN take turns executing one (atomic) statement at a time.
Your program will execute the steps of the algorithm, while SPIN will remain in the loop defined by **goto** T0_init as long as mutex is true. When
your program finally enters a state in which mutex is false, the nondeterministic **if**-statement can choose the first alternative and jump to the label
accept_all. **skip** is not really a statement, so SPIN has successfully terminated its program (the never claim). The program that terminates first
is defined to have"won" the game. The never claim terminates in a state
in which mutex is false, showing <>!mutex is true; by duality (Section 5.6)
<>!mutex is equivalent to ![]mutex, thus falsifying your correctness specifi-
cation, []mutex.

Suppose now that your algorithm is correct and that mutual exclusion
does hold for every possible computation. Then SPIN will never be able to
complete the computation of the claim (which is why it was called a never
claim). The search will terminate and SPIN will not win because it cannot find
a computation in which ![]mutex is true. If we unravel the double negation,
![]mutex is not true so []mutex is true, and the verifier reports that there are
no errors. You win!

Advanced: "Executing" a never claim

The above description is somewhat misleading since the game is
not played by "executing" the programs as in simulation mode, but
rather it describes what happens in verification mode, which involves a search of the entire state space. If mutual exclusion does
not hold, eventually a computation will be found in which the nondeterminism is resolved by choosing the alternative guarded by
(!((mutex))). The end of the never claim has been reached and SPIN
wins the game.

10.3.2 A never claim for a liveness property

Consider now the liveness property <>csp. SPIN wins the game if it can find
a computation in which !<>csp holds. By duality, !<>csp is equivalent to
[]!csp, so the formula cannot be falsified by finding a single state in which
!csp is true (as was the case with !mutex); instead, SPIN must find an infinite
computation in which !csp is true in all states, similar to the one shown in
Figure 10.1.

The never claim for !<>csp is:

```
never  { /* !(<>csp) */
accept_init:
T0_init:
   if
   :: (! ((csp))) -> goto T0_init
   fi;
}
```

The game is played as before, with you and SPIN alternating turns. For this never claim, there are two possibilities: If csp ever becomes true, SPIN is blocked in its **if**-statement because there are no alternatives to (!((csp))), and blocking is considered a loss for SPIN. A computation that contains a state in which csp is true has been found, so the computation cannot falsify []!csp. You win and the verifier reports no errors.

If, on the other hand, csp never becomes true, SPIN will loop forever at the never claim; it repeatedly executes the **if**-statement labeled accept_init. A computation of a never claim that *infinitely often* passes through a statement whose label begins with accept is called an *acceptance cycle*. If a verification finds an acceptance cycle, it is considered a win for SPIN. This acceptance cycle shows that there is an infinite computation in which !csp is always true, that is, []!csp is true. By duality, this is equivalent to !<>csp, so <>csp is false and you lose the game.

The acceptance cycle is written to the trail so that you can examine the counterexample to find the error (see Section 5.4.2).

The term *acceptance cycle* explains why in Section 5.4.2 on verifying liveness properties, we required that the word Acceptance be selected in the JSPIN toolbar or the argument -a be used with pan on the command line.

10.3.3 Never claims for other LTL formulas

As mentioned in Section 5.9.2, it is unlikely that you will want to prove just <>csp because the specification of the liveness property of absence of starvation requires that if a process *ever* tries to enter the critical section it will eventually succeed. A better correctness specification is the formula for infinitely often, []<>csp; the negation of the formula is ![]<>csp, which by duality is equivalent to <>[]!csp. That is, the cycle showing []!csp need not begin in the initial state. The formula ![]<>csp translates into the following never claim:

```
never { /* !([]<>csp) */
T0_init:
   if
   :: (! ((csp))) -> goto accept_S4
   :: (1) -> goto T0_init
   fi;

accept_S4:
   if
   :: (! ((csp))) -> goto accept_S4
   fi;
}
```

The acceptance cycle need not start with the first occurrence of !csp; instead, the computation can take the alternative guarded by (1) indefinitely and only later jump to accept_S4 to start the acceptance cycle.

For completeness, let us look at the never claim for the negation of the latching formula <>[]csp. The negated formula !<>[]csp is equivalent to []<>!csp; a counterexample must have csp become false infinitely often so that it does not become latched to true. The formula is translated to following never claim:

```
never { /* !(<>[]csp) */
T0_init:
   if
   :: (! ((csp))) -> goto accept_S9
   :: (1) -> goto T0_init
   fi;
accept_S9:
   if
   :: (1) -> goto T0_init
   fi;
}
```

As before, the search for a counterexample to <>!csp can start after an arbitrary prefix. When some state is found in which csp is false, <>!csp is true. Control returns to the start of the never claim so that it can search for another instance of <>!csp, which is required to show that []<>!csp holds.

10.3.4 Predefined constructs for use in never claims

Some predefined variables and functions are used only in never claims:

- The predefined variable **_last** is read-only and global; its value is the process ID of the last process from which a statement was executed.
- The predefined function **pc_value** returns an integer representing the current location counter of the process whose ID is given as a parameter to the function.
- The predefined boolean function **enabled** returns true if and only if the process whose ID is given as a parameter to the function has an executable statement.
- The predefined boolean variable **np_** is read-only and global; its value is true in all states that are not *progress states* as defined in Section 10.4.

Remote references enable access from within a never claim to the current location counter of a process or the current value of a local variable (Section 5.7).

10.4 Non-progress cycles

SPIN has the capability to verify some liveness properties without writing a correctness specification in temporal logic. Consider, for example, an algorithm that solves the critical section problem and fulfils the liveness property of absence of starvation. What this means is that *any* (infinite) computation of the algorithm must pass through the critical section of all of the processes infinitely often.[3] A counterexample to this correctness specification would be an infinite computation that manages to avoid the critical section of some process.

Listing 10.3 shows an algorithm that solves the critical section problem for three processes using semaphores (Section 4.5). Let us select an arbitrary process, say P, and designate the critical section as a *progress* state by labeling it with a label that begins with the string progress (lines 6–7). What would it mean for process P to be starved? By the structure of the program, it is clear that that could occur only if there were a computation in which the P ceases to execute statements, so that the remainder of the computation includes only statements from other two processes. In other words, the correctness specification can be falsified only if there is an infinite computation that does not include *infinitely many* occurrences of the progress state. In SPIN this is called

---

[3] This assumes that processes do not halt in their noncritical sections.

Listing 10.3. Non-progress cycles

```
 1  byte sem = 1;
 2
 3  active proctype P() {
 4    do
 5    :: atomic { sem > 0 ; sem = sem - 1 }
 6  progress:
 7        sem = sem + 1
 8    od
 9  }
10  active proctype Q() {
11    do
12    :: atomic { sem > 0 ; sem = sem - 1 }
13        sem = sem + 1
14    od
15  }
16  active proctype R() {
17    do
18    :: atomic { sem > 0 ; sem = sem - 1 }
19        sem = sem + 1
20    od
21  }
```

a *non-progress cycle*, because eventually the computation enters a cycle that does not contain a progress state. To search for a non-progress cycle:

jSpin

Select Non-progress from the pulldown menu. Select Verify to run SPIN and then Trail to view the cycle if one is found.

Command line

The generated verifier must be compiled with the argument –DNP and the verifier run with the argument –l:

```
spin -a sem-prog.pml
gcc -DNP -o pan pan.c
pan -l
```

SPIN quickly reports an error and a guided simulation shows that there is an infinite computation in which only processes Q and R participate:

```
2 R        20   sem>0
2 R        20   sem = (sem-1)
Process Statement                   sem
2 R        21   sem = (sem+1)   0
1 Q        13   sem>0           1
1 Q        13   sem = (sem-1)   1
1 Q        14   sem = (sem+1)   0
2 R        20   sem>0           1
2 R        20   sem = (sem-1)   1
2 R        21   sem = (sem+1)   0
<<<<<START OF CYCLE>>>>>
2 R        20   sem>0           1
2 R        20   sem = (sem-1)   1
2 R        21   sem = (sem+1)   0
1 Q        13   sem>0           1
1 Q        13   sem = (sem-1)   1
1 Q        14   sem = (sem+1)   0
2 R        20   sem>0           1
2 R        20   sem = (sem-1)   1
2 R        21   sem = (sem+1)   0
```

Although the guard sem>0 is true infinitely often, the search always chooses a transition from Q (line 12) or R (line 18), instead of the one from P (line 5). Therefore, process P experiences starvation.

Run a verification with non-progress cycles for Peterson's algorithm (Listing 5.4); there will be no errors because starvation is impossible in that algorithm.

Non-progress cycle are implemented by generating a never claim using the predefined variable **np_** that is true if no process is at a progress state. There is a non-progress cycle if there is an acceptance cycle in which **np_** is always true.

11

Case Studies*

This chapter contains five case studies designed to bring together the individual programming structures in PROMELA and the SPIN verification techniques that we have studied in isolation. The first case study shows how to create data structures using channels together with the various send and receive statements. In the second case study we show how to program two classic nondeterministic algorithms. The third and fourth case studies model a scheduling algorithm and a mutual exclusion algorithm for real-time systems. The final case study examines an algorithm for a distributed system. It shows that a model for verifying a distributed system need not be constructed according the system architecture; instead, a more efficient model can be constructed that captures the algorithmic behavior of the system.

11.1 Channels as data structures

While channels are intended to be used for modeling communications lines, the statements defined on channels are quite flexible and can be used to implement data structures that are otherwise impossible to implement in PROMELA. Listing 6.2 presented an implementation of sparse arrays that used an array to hold the entries for non-zero elements. Here, a different implementation is given: the entries are stored in channels and the program is expanded to add two sparse arrays.

The **inline** construct (Section 6.4) will be used extensively to structure the program. Recall that **inline** simply performs textual substitution without creating a new scope, so declarations are usually written outside the inlined code to prevent multiple declarations. Listing 11.1 contains the main process, where two sparse arrays sa1 and sa2 are initialized and printed

Listing 11.1. Sparse arrays (main program)

```
1   active proctype P() {
2     int i;
3     ENTRY e, e1, e2;
4
5     initEntry(sa1, 0, 1, -5);
6     initEntry(sa1, 0, 3, 8);
7     initEntry(sa1, 2, 0, 20);
8     initEntry(sa1, 3, 3, -3);
9     printf("Sparse array 1:\n");
10    printSA(sa1);
11
12    initEntry(sa2, 0, 2, -2);
13    initEntry(sa2, 0, 3, 5);
14    initEntry(sa2, 2, 0, -15);
15    printf("Sparse array 2:\n");
16    printSA(sa2);
17
18    addSA(sa1, sa2, sa3);
19    printf("Sparse array 3:\n");
20    printSA(sa3)
21  }
```

(lines 5–10 and 12–16); then the code for adding the arrays into sparse array sa3 is called and the result is printed (lines 18–20).

Listing 11.2 contains the global declarations of the program. The entries in the sparse array are defined to be of a type declared in a **typedef** (lines 1–5), and channels are declared to store the entries (lines 7–9). The initialization of the arrays is easier than it was before, because once an entry is built (lines 12–14), an output statement S!e places the entry into the channel (lines 15), and there is no need to keep track of the current index in an array.

The code for printing a sparse array (Listing 11.3) is interesting. We want to read the values of all the entries in the channel, without destroying the data structure as would happen if we executed an ordinary receive statement that removes a message from the channel:

```
do
:: nempty(S) -> S ? e; printf(...)
:: empty(S)  -> break
od
```

Listing 11.2. Sparse arrays (declarations)

```
1   typedef ENTRY {
2     byte row;
3     byte col;
4     int value
5   }
6
7   chan sa1 = [ 5] of { ENTRY };
8   chan sa2 = [ 5] of { ENTRY };
9   chan sa3 = [10] of { ENTRY };
10
11  inline initEntry(S, R, C, V) {
12    e.row = R;
13    e.col = C;
14    e.value = V;
15    S ! e
16  }
```

The trick is to immediately send back to the channel every entry that we receive (lines 6–7); at the end of the loop the channel returns to its original state. How do we know when the loop is finished? The number of messages in the channel (Section 7.4.1) is assigned to a variable i that is used to count down from its initial value **len**(S) to zero (lines 2, 4, 10).

The algorithm for adding two sparse arrays (Listing 11.4) assumes that they are sorted; it is very similar to the algorithm for merging sorted lists. There are four alternatives in the **do**-statement, depending on which channels are *nonempty*: (a) neither (line 3); (b) the first channel only (lines 4–9); (c) the second channel only (lines 10–15); or (d) both (lines 16–29).

- If both channels are empty, the algorithm can terminate.
- If only one channel is nonempty, we transfer its contents to the result channel sa3 (lines 6, 12). **do**-statements are used, and the second alternatives are chosen when the channel is empty in order to break the loop.
- If both channels are nonempty, the algorithm must examine three cases: (a) the heads of both channels refer to the same array element (lines 20–23); (b) the head of the first channel refers to a smaller element than the head of the second (lines 24–26); and (c) otherwise, the second channel holds the smaller element (lines 27–28).

Listing 11.3. Sparse arrays (printing)

```
1   inline printSA(S) {
2     i = len(S);
3     do
4     :: i == 0 -> break
5     :: else ->
6          S ? e;
7          S ! e;
8          printf("Row = %d, column = %d, value = %d\n",
9             e.row, e.col, e.value)
10         i--
11    od
12  }
```

To determine which alternative holds we need the values of the entries at the heads of *both* channels, but in the second and third alternatives we only use one of them and the other should be "pushed back" onto the head of the channel. In PROMELA a message cannot be pushed back onto the head of a channel, but we can obtain the values of the entries at the head of the channels without actually removing them from the channel by copying their values (Section 7.7) as shown in lines 17–18.

An **if**-statement determines what to do in each case: (a) remove both entries and use initEntry to create a new entry with the sum of the values of the two; (b–c) transfer the entry from one of the channels to the result channel. The following drawing shows in bold the element that will be appended to the sa3 after removing the heads of the other two channels and adding their values:

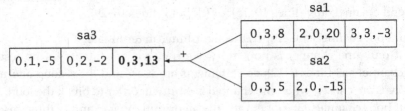

Listing 11.4. Sparse arrays (adding)

```
1   inline addSA(S1, S2, S3) {
2     do
3     :: empty(S1) && empty(S2) -> break
4     :: nempty(S1) && empty(S2) ->
5         do
6         :: nempty(S1) -> S1 ? e1; S3 ! e1
7         :: empty(S1) -> break
8         od;
9         break
10    :: empty(S1) && nempty(S2) ->
11        do
12        :: nempty(S2) -> S2 ? e2; S3 ! e2
13        :: empty(S2) -> break
14        od;
15        break
16    :: nempty(S1) && nempty(S2) ->
17        S1 ? <e1>;
18        S2 ? <e2>;
19        if
20        :: (e1.row == e2.row) && (e1.col == e2.col) ->
21            S1 ? e1;
22            S2 ? e2;
23            initEntry(S3, e1.row, e1.col, e1.value+e2.value)
24        :: (e1.row < e2.row) ||
25           ((e1.row == e2.row) && (e1.col < e2.col)) ->
26            S1 ? e1; S3 ! e1
27        :: else ->
28            S2 ? e2; S3 ! e2
29        fi
30    od
31  }
```

11.2 Nondeterministic algorithms

The first article on nondeterministic *algorithms* was written by Robert W. Floyd in 1967 [10]. Floyd regarded nondeterminism as a concise way of expressing algorithms that could be mechanically translated into deterministic algorithms that use backtracking. Forty years later, it is appropriate to write these algorithms as PROMELA programs and to obtain solutions using the automatic backtracking performed during a SPIN verification. The algorithms and notation from [10] will be retained. Code for initializing and printing data has been omitted and can be found in the software archive.

The first algorithm is the classic eight-queens problem that you have almost certainly encountered. The second is less well known: finding all simple cycles in a directed graph.

11.2.1 The eight-queens problem

The eight-queens problem is to write an algorithm to place eight queens on an 8×8 chessboard so that no queen can capture any other. A solution is shown in Figure 11.1.

Floyd's algorithm written in PROMELA is given in Listing 11.5. A solution to the problem is an array of eight integer values stored in the variable result; for each *column* i, result[i] is the *row* in which the queen is placed,

Fig. 11.1. A solution to the eight-queens problem

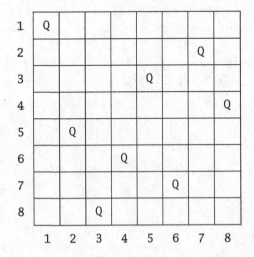

Listing 11.5. The eight-queens problem

```
1   byte result[8];
2   bool a[8];
3   bool b[15];
4   bool c[15];
5
6   active proctype Queens() {
7     byte col = 1;
8     byte row;
9     do
10    :: Choose();
11       !a[row-1];
12       !b[row+col-2];
13       !c[row-col+7];
14       a[row-1]  = true;
15       b[row+col-2] = true;
16       c[row-col+7] = true;
17       result[col-1] = row;
18       if
19       :: col == 8 -> break
20       :: else  -> col++
21       fi
22    od;
23    Write()
24  }
```

so for the solution in Figure 11.1, result contains $1, 5, 8, 6, 3, 7, 2, 4$. The algorithm works by nondeterministically choosing a row for each column in sequence, and then checking that a queen placed on that square cannot capture a queen that has already been placed on the board.

To facilitate checking for captures, three auxiliary boolean arrays are used: a[i] is true if there is a queen in row i; b[i] is true if there is a queen on the positive diagonal i; c[i] is true if there is a queen on the negative diagonal i. The positive diagonals go from the lower left to the upper right of the board, while the negative diagonals go from the upper left to the lower right. It is easy to check that there are fifteen diagonals of each type, that the squares on the positive diagonals are those with equal values of the sum of the row and column numbers, and that the squares on the negative diagonals are those with equal values of the difference between them.

The process starts out by initializing col to 1. It then proceeds with a **do**-statement that places a queen on each column in sequence, terminating when a queen has been placed on the eighth column (lines 18–21). The nondeterministic choice of a row for each column is done in an inline sequence Choose (not shown), which is implemented as a nondeterministic **if**-statement using the technique shown in Section 4.6.2.

Once a row number is chosen for a queen, lines 11–13 check the row and diagonal data structures to see if a capture is possible. If so, the execution blocks, and since there is only one process, the computation terminates at this point. If a capture is not possible, the data structures are updated (lines 14–16) and the row number stored in result. Since array indices in PROMELA start from zero, offsets to the indices must be computed in lines 11–17. Once all queens have been placed successfully, the solution is written out in the inline sequence Write.

There is not much point in running a random simulation of this algorithm. The vast majority of the computations of the program end with the process Queens blocked because one queen can capture another. You can run an interactive simulation if you know a solution, but, of course, the whole point is to have the program compute one.

A SPIN verification can be run to search for a solution. Add the assertion

assert(**false**)

as the last statement of the program. A counterexample for the verification will be one in which the assertion is violated, namely, a computation that successfully exits the loop because all queens have been placed on the board.

However, there is one problem with the verification. Whenever the process is blocked because one queen can capture another, the process is at an end state, but it is an invalid one that is not the final statement of the process (Section 4.7.2). To enable the verifier to continue the search for a counterexample violating the assertion, labels starting with the string end can be added to lines 11, 12, and 13:

```
enda:  !a[row-1];
endb:  !b[row+col-2];
endc:  !b[row-col+7];
```

Alternatively, run the verifier with the –E argument.

The verifier reports an assertion violation and running a guided simulation with the trail file prints a solution to the problem:

```
   1,    5,    8,    6,    3,    7,    2,    4,
spin: line   47 "queens.pml", Error: assertion violated
spin: text of failed assertion: assert(0)
spin: trail ends after 105 steps
```

At the end of a simulation, SPIN prints the details of the final state: the values of the location counters and the variables. If you are interested just in the output from the **printf** statements, the printout of the final state can be suppressed by using the –B argument.

It is well known that the eight-queens problem has 92 solutions. As described in Section 8.1.3, it is possible to request that the verifier find all of them:

```
pan -E -c0 -e
```

Contrary to our expectation, the program in Listing 11.5 will find only 86 out of the 92 counterexamples. The problem is that the variable result is *write-only* because it is assigned to in line 17, but its value is never read:

```
spin: warning, "queens.pml",
     global, 'byte  result' variable is never used
```

The verifier generated by SPIN optimizes its search by ignoring write-only variables since they cannot affect the correctness of a correctness specification. **printf** statements are also ignored during verifications, so the variable result is not "read" in this program.

All 92 solutions can be generated by artificially reading the value of result; add the statement

```
byte dummy = result[0]
```

after the **do**-statement and before the **assert** statement. Of course, a warning message will be issued that dummy is write-only, but we are not interested in its value. If the anonymous write-only variable is used, there will be no warning message:

```
_ = result[0]
```

11.2.2 Cycles in a directed graph

Consider the directed graph in Figure 11.2. The path defined by the sequence of nodes (1,3,2,4) returning the first node 1 is a *simple cycle*: it is a closed path that does not go through any node more than once. The problem is to write an algorithm to find simple cycles in a directed graph.

Fig. 11.2. Simple cycles in a directed graph

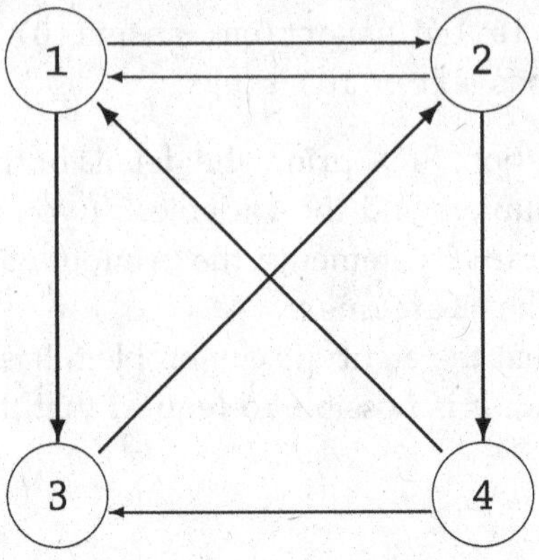

Floyd's algorithm uses a two-dimensional array *step* to store the directed graph, where $step_{i,j}$ is true if and only if there is an edge from node i to node j. The implementation in PROMELA is shown in Listing 11.6. The two-dimensional array step is implemented using **typedef** (lines 1–6). The boolean array used ensures that a node appears at most once in a cycle; used[i] is true if and only if node i has been used. The list of nodes in a cycle is stored in the array result (line 8).

Nodes are chosen nondeterministically as described in Section 4.6.2. Once an initial node is chosen (line 13), a **do**-statement is executed until a new node has been chosen that is the same as the initial node (line 22). The variable old is used to store the last node chosen (lines 14, 25). The body of the loop consists of storing old in result (line 16), nondeterministically choosing a new node (line 18), and checking that this node has not been used before (line 19) and that there is an edge from the old node to the new one (line 20). If so, we mark the node as used (line 24) and prepare for the next execution of the loop (line 25).

Running a verification to find solutions proceeds exactly as described in the previous subsection for the eight-queens algorithm. There are 15 solutions for the graph in Figure 11.2, which consist of all cyclic shifts of

```
(1, 2)
(1, 2, 4)
(1, 3, 2)
(1, 3, 2, 4)
(2, 4, 3)
```

Listing 11.6. Cycles in a directed graph

```
1   #define N 4
2   typedef ROW {
3     bool row[N];
4   }
5
6   ROW step[N];
7   bool used[N];
8   byte result[N];
9
10  active proctype Cycles() {
11    byte initial, old, new, i;
12    initValues();
13    Choose(initial);
14    old = initial;
15    do
16    :: result[i] = old;
17       i++;
18       Choose(new);
19       !used[new-1];
20       step[old-1].row[new-1];
21       if
22       :: new == initial -> break
23       :: else ->
24          used[new-1] = true;
25          old = new
26       fi
27    od;
28    Write();
29    assert(false)
30  }
```

11.3 Modeling a real-time scheduling algorithm

SPIN is intended to be used to model and verify concurrent and distributed systems without the use of numeric values of time and duration. Algorithms for these systems are designed to be independent of the speed of execution of a process or the speed at which a message is delivered, so it is sufficient to know that there are no errors caused by interleaving statements and messages. SPIN can model real-time systems by treating time as discrete so that it can be represented by a variable of integer type. In this section we model a scheduling algorithm and verify that it is correct.

11.3.1 Real-time systems

Real-time systems are those that have requirements on their response times.[1] For example, a flight control system is required to sample sensors and issue appropriate commands to the flight controls every t milliseconds, where t ranges from 5 to 50 milliseconds. Real-time systems are constructed by dividing up the computation into short *tasks* and then *scheduling* the tasks. The scheduling may be synchronous, where each task is given one or more slots within a period of time, or asynchronous, where the tasks are given priorities and a preemptive scheduler ensures that a lower-priority task is not run if a higher-priority task is ready.

Tasks in a real-time system are generally defined to be *periodic*: with each task we associate a *period* p and an *execution time* e. The task is required to execute at least once every p units of time (microseconds or milliseconds or seconds), and it needs at most e units to complete its execution. Consider, for example, two tasks T_0 and T_1, such that $p_0 = 2, e_0 = 1$, and $p_1 = 5, e_1 = 2$; that is, T_0 needs 1 unit out of every 2 units, and T_1 needs 2 units out of every 5. We now ask if there is a *feasible* assignment of priorities, that is, if there is an assignment of priorities such that each task receives the execution time it requires when the tasks are scheduled by an asynchronous scheduler.

The following diagram shows that assigning T_0 a higher priority than T_1 is feasible:[2]

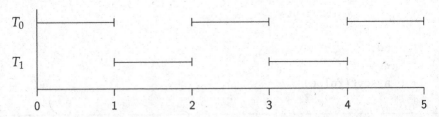

T_0 receives the first unit out of every two. The execution of T_1 starts at time 1 and is interrupted at time 2 because the higher priority task T_0 is now ready to execute. Task T_1 resumes execution at time 3. In total, T_1 receives two units out of every five as required.

---

[1] An introduction to real-time systems can be found in Chapter 13 of *PCDP*. A comprehensive reference is [14].

[2] These diagrams are taken from Section 13.12 of *PCDP* and are used with the permission of Pearson Education.

Not all assignments are feasible. Assigning a higher priority to T_1 results in the computation shown in the following diagram:

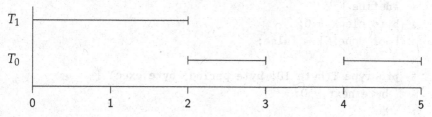

T_1 executes for two units without interruption, by which time T_0 has not received one unit out of the two that it needs.

We now show how to model an asynchronous scheduler of periodic tasks in PROMELA. When no priorities are assigned, the scheduler will contain errors because the requirements will not be met. Then we model preemptive scheduling with priorities using a scheduling algorithm that produces a feasible assignment if one exists.

11.3.2 Modeling a scheduler in PROMELA

A model of a scheduler without priorities is shown in Listing 11.7. The global variable clock models time. Each task T receives as parameters an identification number, its period, and its execution time (line 5). Since we need not execute a task more often than its period, the task is executable only if the clock has reached its next scheduled time (line 9). The execution of the task is modeled by adding the task's execution time exec to the clock (line 10); then, the next time to run the task is computed (line 11). Finally, a global flag done is set (line 12).

This flag is used to implement a watchdog (see Section 8.1.1). There is a task Watchdog corresponding to each task T. Each task is required to set its flag by the end of its deadline (line 21). The watchdog is executed when the clock has passed the deadline for T; the deadline is one period later than the next time at which the task is to be executed (lines 18, 23). If the flag has not been set, the **assert** statement (line 22) will cause an error.

Since the periodic tasks may not take all of the available execution time, a task Idle is used to increment the variable clock if no other process can be executed (lines 1–7 of Listing 11.8). The initial process instantiates the processes with their parameters (lines 9–17 of Listing 11.8).

Running simulations leads to errors when the assertion is evaluated and found to be false. The value of clock in several runs ranged from 5 to 20.

Listing 11.7. Periodic execution of tasks

```
1   #define N 2
2   byte clock = 0;
3   bool done[N] = false;
4
5   proctype T(byte ID; byte period; byte exec) {
6     byte next = 0;
7     do
8     :: atomic {
9          clock >= next ->
10             clock = clock + exec;
11             next = next + period;
12             done[ID] = true
13        }
14     od
15  }
16
17  proctype Watchdog(byte ID; byte period) {
18    byte deadline = period;
19    do
20    :: atomic {
21         clock >= deadline ->
22            assert done[ID];
23            deadline = deadline + period;
24            done[ID] = false
25       }
26    od
27  }
```

An attempt to verify the model leads to a short counterexample as shown by the following guided simulation (edited from the display of JSPIN):

```
Process Statement                 T(4):next clock done[0] done[1]
4 T      9   clock>=next
4 T     10   clock = (clock+exec)
4 T     11   next = (next+period) 2
4 T     12   done[ID] = 1          5        2
3 Watch 21   clock>=deadline       5        2      0       1
spin: line  22 "sched1.pml", Error: assertion violated
spin: text of failed assertion: assert(done[ID])
```

Listing 11.8. Idle and initial processes

```
1  proctype Idle() {
2    do
3    :: atomic {
4          timeout -> clock++
5        }
6    od
7  }
8
9  init {
10   atomic {
11     run Idle();
12     run T(0, 2, 1);
13     run Watchdog(0, 2);
14     run T(1, 5, 2);
15     run Watchdog(1, 5)
16   }
17 }
```

This guided simulation is the incorrect computation shown in the diagram on page 175, where T_1 is scheduled before T_0. The process T with **pid** 4 models T_1 and is executed first, followed by process Watchdog with **pid** 3 that models the watchdog associated with T_0. It detects that the deadline for T_0 has arrived but its done flag is not set.

11.3.3 Simplifying the model

The model can be simplified by combining both the task T and its watchdog into one process (Listing 11.9). A guarded command is used to choose between the processing of the task (lines 6–11) and the watchdog (lines 12–17). We have added an additional term to the guard of the task (line 7) to ensure that once the deadline has passed the watchdog will be executed, not the task. The Idle and initial tasks remain as shown in Listing 11.8.

11.3.4 Modeling a scheduler with priorities

In Section 9.3 we introduced two constructs in PROMELA for modeling priorities. The specifier **priority** is not relevant here because it just affects the

Listing 11.9. Periodic execution of tasks (simplified)

```
1  proctype T(byte ID; byte period; byte exec) {
2    byte next = 0;
3    byte deadline = period;
4    bool done = false;
5    do
6    :: atomic {
7        (clock >= next) && (clock < deadline) ->
8            clock = clock + exec;
9            next = next + period;
10           done = true
11     }
12   :: atomic {
13        clock >= deadline ->
14            assert done;
15            deadline = deadline + period;
16            done = false
17     }
18   od
19 }
```

relative priority of processes in simulation and cannot be used to verify properties of a preemptive scheduler. The specifier **provided** enables absolute priority to be given to one process over another and could have been used, but instead, we will model priority directly.

The model for the priority-driven scheduler is shown in Listing 11.10. (The Idle and initial processes are straightforward and are shown in Listing 11.11.) The priorities are modeled by a queue implemented by a channel that is used to store the tasks (line 4). The messages in the channel are the IDs of the tasks, and tasks with lower IDs are assumed to have higher priority. By storing the IDs in ascending order we ensure that the message at the head of the channel is of the highest priority.

When a task must be executed (clock>=next, line 13), it places its ID on the queue (lines 16); the guard in line 15

```
!(queue ?? [eval(ID)])
```

ensures that a task is not queued if it is already in the channel. The double question marks check if the argument can be matched anywhere on the channel and not just at the head. The brackets denote side-effect-free polling, and

Listing 11.10. Scheduling with priorities

```
1   #define MAX 4
2   byte clock = 0;
3   byte maxPeriod;
4   chan queue = [MAX] of { byte };
5
6   proctype T(byte ID; byte period; byte exec) {
7     byte next = 0;
8     byte deadline = period;
9     byte current = 0;
10  end:
11    do
12    :: atomic {
13        (clock >= next) && (clock < deadline) &&
14        (clock < maxPeriod) &&
15        !(queue ?? [eval(ID)]) ->
16          queue !! ID
17      }
18    :: atomic {
19        (clock >= next) && (clock < deadline) &&
20        (queue ? [eval(ID)]) ->
21          current++;
22          clock++;
23          if
24          :: current == exec ->
25              queue ? eval(ID);
26              current = 0;
27              next = next + period
28          :: else
29          fi
30      }
31    :: atomic {
32        (clock >= deadline) ->
33          assert (!(queue ?? [eval(ID)]));
34          deadline = deadline + period
35      }
36    od
37  }
```

Listing 11.11. Idle and initial processes

```
1   proctype Idle() {
2   end:
3     do
4     :: atomic {
5           (clock < maxPeriod) && timeout ->
6               clock++
7         }
8     od
9   }
10
11  init {
12    atomic {
13      run Idle();
14      maxPeriod = 5;
15      queue ! 0;
16      queue ! 1;
17      run T(0, 2, 1);
18      run T(1, 5, 2);
19    }
20  }
```

eval computes the current value of the variable ID for the match. We also check that clock < deadline (line 13) so that a task is not placed on queue once its deadline has passed. The term in line 14 of the guard is explained below.

The second alternative (lines 18–30) models the execution of a task. It is executable under the same conditions on clock as the previous alternative, together with the condition that the task's ID is on the head of the queue (line 20). To enable preemption we no longer add the value of exec to clock; instead, clock is incremented by one unit of time (line 22), as is the variable current which keeps track of how many units have been executed by this task (line 21). If the execution time of the task has completed (current==exec, line 24), the variable current is reset (line 26) and the time when the task must be executed next is computed (line 27).

The array of flags done is not needed to implement a watchdog; instead, the channel is checked to see if the task ID is still there (lines 31–35).

To implement priorities, *sorted send* is used (line 16). The double exclamation point causes the message to be inserted into the channel in sorted order. The poll statement (line 20) and the receive statement (line 25) check and remove the message at the head of the channel, ensuring that priorities are implemented as intended.

It can be shown that if a counterexample exists, then one exists within the initial part of the computation defined by the first period of some task [14, Section 6.5]. Therefore, it is sufficient to verify the model for values of clock up to the maximum of the periods; this is stored in the variable maxPeriod and set in the initial process (line 14 of Listing 11.11). The alternative that adds a task to the queue (line 14 of Listing 11.10) and the alternative that increments clock (line 5 of Listing 11.11) become unexecutable when the value of maxPeriod is reached. The labels end (line 10 of Listing 11.10 and line 2 of Listing 11.11) prevent the reporting of invalid end states.

A verification for the two tasks T_0, T_1 initialized in lines 17–18 of Listing 11.11 will not report any errors, but if the initialization is changed such that the IDs of the tasks are exchanged:

```
run T(1, 2, 1);
run T(0, 5, 2);
```

a counterexample will be found.

11.3.5 Rate monotonic scheduling

It can be shown that if there is a feasible priority assignment, then *rate monotonic scheduling* is feasible [14, Section 6.4]. This is achieved by assigning priorities in inverse order of the *periods* of the tasks, that is, the shorter the period, the higher the priority. This is the reason that task T_0 of the example was given a higher priority. The reader is invited to experiment with the following data in order to see which have feasible priority assignments and which do not:[3]

$$(p_1 = 8, e_1 = 3), (p_2 = 9, e_2 = 3), (p_3 = 15, e_3 = 3),$$
$$(p_1 = 8, e_1 = 4), (p_2 = 12, e_2 = 4), (p_3 = 20, e_3 = 4),$$
$$(p_1 = 8, e_1 = 4), (p_2 = 10, e_2 = 2), (p_3 = 12, e_3 = 3).$$

11.4 Fischer's algorithm

This section shows another example of the use of discrete time in a model. The example is Fischer's algorithm for solving the critical section problem

---

[3] The data are taken from Exercise 6.5 in [14].

Listing 11.12. An algorithm for the critical section problem

```
1   #define N 6
2   byte turn = 0;
3
4   active [N] proctype P() {
5     do
6     :: turn == 0 ->
7            turn = _pid+1;
8            turn == _pid+1 ->
9                /* Critical section */
10               turn = 0
11    od
12  }
```

[15, Section 24.2]. Although the algorithm is very efficient, its correctness depends on the actual time taken by each statement, so its use should be limited primarily to systems, such as real-time systems, in which timing constraints are an essential part of their design.

Consider the algorithm for the critical section problem show in Listing 11.12. The variable turn is used to indicate if a process is trying to enter its critical section and its value is zero if none is doing so. The expression in line 8 is supposed to ensure that if process has set the variable, then no other process has subsequently set it to another value.

Of course, the algorithm is trivially incorrect, as shown in the following computation in which mutual exclusion is not achieved:

Process	Statement	turn
P1	turn == 0	0
P2	turn == 0	0
P1	turn = 1	0
P1	turn == 1	1
P1	/* CS */	1
P2	turn = 2	1
P2	turn == 2	2
P2	/* CS */	2

Consider now a computation that starts as follows:

Process	Statement	turn
P1	turn == 0	0
P1	turn = 1	0
P2	turn == 0	1
P1	turn == 1	1

In this computation, P1 "quickly" sets its ID in turn after discovering that turn is zero, and then "slowly" rechecks the value of turn so that P2 has a chance to execute and to become blocked when it finds that turn is not zero. It can be shown that if the duration of "slowly" is at least as great as that of "quickly," the algorithm is correct.

A PROMELA program for Fischer's algorithm is shown in Listings 11.13 and 11.14. The algorithm in Listing 11.13 is the same as at that in Listing 11.12, except that we have added an array variable timer (line 6) to implement the delays described above. The guard in line 16 ensures that a process sets its ID in turn *within* DELAY1 time units of finding out that turn is zero (line 12). The guard in line 23 ensures that a process *checks* its ID in turn (line 25) *at least* DELAY2 time units after it *sets* its ID in turn (line 17–18). **atomic** is used extensively to prevent interleaving between setting or checking the timers and the corresponding actions of the algorithm.

A separate process is used to model a ticking clock (Listing 11.14). In one deterministic step, it decrements all timers that have positive values. The Clock process is executed *asynchronously* with the processes in Listing 11.13. If Clock is not executed between line 12 and line 16 of one of the processes P, the computation models the case in which line 16 is executed immediately after line 12. If Clock is executed three times between line 12 and line 16, the computation models the case in which P waited "too long" (greater than DELAY1 units) between the statements. timer[_pid] will have been decremented to zero and the attempt to enter the critical section is abandoned (line 19).

If all processes P are blocked at line 23 with nonzero timers, the process Clock will be the only one that is executable; when it decrements the values of one or more timers to zero, some of the other processes will no longer be blocked.

Listing 11.13. Fischer's algorithm for the critical section problem

```
1  #define N 6
2  #define DELAY1 2
3  #define DELAY2 3
4
5  byte turn = 0;
6  byte timer[N] = 0;
7
8  active [N] proctype P() {
9  start:
10   do
11   :: atomic {
12         turn == 0 -> timer[_pid] = DELAY1
13       }
14     atomic {
15       if
16       :: timer[_pid] > 0 ->
17             turn = _pid+1;
18             timer[_pid] = DELAY2
19       :: else -> goto start
20       fi
21     }
22     atomic {
23         timer[_pid] == 0 ->
24           if
25           :: turn == _pid+1
26           :: else -> goto start
27           fi
28     }
29     atomic {
30       /* Critical section */
31       turn = 0
32     }
33   od
34 }
```

Listing 11.14. Modeling a clock for Fischer's algorithm

```
1  active proctype Clock() {
2    byte i;
3    do
4    :: d_step {
5        i = 0;
6        do
7        :: i >= N -> break
8        :: else ->
9            if
10           :: timer[i] > 0 -> timer[i]--
11           :: else
12           fi;
13           i++
14       od
15       }
16   od
17 }
```

Mutual exclusion is verified as usual by incrementing a variable critical and asserting that it is at most one. Replace lines 22–32 in Listing 11.13 by

```
atomic {
    timer[_pid] == 0 ->
        if
        :: (turn == _pid+1) -> critical++;
        :: else -> goto start
        fi
}
atomic {
    assert (critical <= 1);
    critical--;
    turn = 0
}
```

The modeling of time and the verification of timing constraints is an important area of current research. DTSPIN is a modified version of SPIN that is optimized for modeling systems using discrete time.[4] Another approach is taken by UPPAAL which is a model checker for timed automata.

11.5 Modeling distributed systems

The final case study concerns distributed systems, which are systems composed of several computers (*nodes*) without access to a common memory; they synchronize and communicate using channels alone. The natural way to model a distributed system in PROMELA is to represent the nodes as processes and the communications channels as channels. We show how to model a distributed algorithm in this manner, and then show how to simplify the model to enable efficient verification.

The nodes of a distributed system are invariably computers that themselves contain multitasking systems. Since there is no structuring construct in PROMELA except for processes, both nodes and processes within the nodes must be modeled by the **proctype** construct. The channels enable synchronization between nodes, so another mechanism like atomic sequences is usually used to synchronize between processes of the same node.

Here we use a different technique for modeling a node: There is a single process for each node and the processes within the nodes are modeled by a nondeterministic **do**-statement. Each time the **do**-statement is executed, one of the alternatives is chosen, and this models the interleaving of the concurrent processes. The advantage of this design is that processes within a node are naturally synchronized with no additional overhead; the disadvantage is that we might miss errors that result when the node is implemented using a lower-level mechanism for synchronization.

The other way in which a PROMELA model can differ from a naive implementation of a distributed system is in its use of channels. Programs with channels require a lot of resources to verify, so models with fewer channels are to be preferred. Therefore, we will associate a single incoming channel with each node, and the process sending a message will pass its identification to the process receiving the message in an additional field. A similar technique was used in some of the models of client-server systems in Sections 7.2 and 7.3.

---

[4] The website for DTSPIN includes a different SPIN model for Fischer's algorithm written by Dragan Bošnački.

11.6 The Chandy–Lamport algorithm for global snapshots

The distributed algorithm that will be modeled and verified is the Chandy–Lamport algorithm for *global snapshots*; a snapshot a set of data giving a *consistent* state of a distributed system. The presentation is divided into three sections: in this section the algorithm is described; Section 11.7 contains a PROMELA implementation of the algorithm, and Section 11.8 shows how to transform the full implementation into a model suitable for verification.

A detailed presentation of the algorithm together with a mathematical proof of its correctness is given in Section 11.4 of *PCDP* and in the original article by Chandy and Lamport [7].

In a system with shared memory, obtaining a snapshot is easy: simply block all the processes and make a copy of the shared memory. The problem with obtaining a snapshot in a distributed system is that the nodes can communicate only by messages, which are not transferred instantly and can take time to move through the channels; it follows that there is no global "bird's-eye" view of the system. If Node 1 sends a message m to Node 2, it is possible for the message to get temporarily "lost" because Node 1 thinks that it had sent the message, while Node 2 doesn't yet know of its existence. A snapshot is *consistent* if it can unambiguously identify every message that has been sent as either *received* or as *still in the channel*.

The Chandy–Lamport algorithm solves the problem by adding a new type of message called a *marker*. Markers are sent by each node over each outgoing channel as a signal that the node has recorded its state. Every message sent *before* the marker "belongs" to either the receiving node or the channel.

The following diagram shows seven messages in a channel between the two nodes:

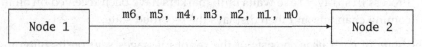

Suppose that the marker has been sent after message m4:

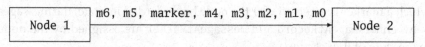

Node 1 records its state as having sent message m0 through m4. It is now the responsibility of Node 2 to record that it has received a subsequence of the messages, say m0 through m2, while the rest of the messages, here m3 and m4, are recorded as being in the channel.

Let us see how Node 2 can record a *subsequence* of the messages as received. Recall that Node 2 may have channels incoming from other nodes such as Node 3. Suppose that Node 2 has received messages m0 through m2 from Node 1, messages n0 and n1 from Node 3, and then receives a marker from Node 3:

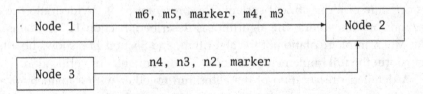

Upon receipt of the marker, Node 2 records its state: messages m0 through m2 received from Node 1 and messages n0 and n1 received from Node 3. When the marker is finally received from Node 1, the state of Node 2 has *already* been recorded, so the messages m3 and m4 have to be identified as belonging to the channel.

The algorithm at each node consists of four processes:

- Process Send message sends messages on an outgoing channel; it records the last message sent on that channel (in a variable lastSent).
- Process Receive message receives messages on an incoming channel and records the last message received (in a variable lastReceived).
- Process Receive marker receives a marker on an incoming channel. First it records the last message that was received on this channel before the marker (in a variable messageAtMarker). Then, if the state has not yet been recorded, the set of messages sent on each outgoing channel is recorded (in a variable stateAtRecord) and the set of messages received on each incoming channel is recorded (in a variable messageAtRecord). Finally, the markers are sent on all outgoing channels.
- Process Display state waits until markers have been received on all incoming channels and then displays the recorded state.

The state of each *node* consists of the set of messages sent on its outgoing channels before it recorded its state, and the set of messages received on its incoming channels before it recorded its state. For each incoming channel on which a marker is received *after* the node has recorded its state, the messages between messageAtRecord and messageAtMarker are assigned by the node to the state of that *channel*.

Figure 11.3 shows the diagram of a distributed system that will be used in the PROMELA models. It consists of three nodes – Node 1, Node 2, Node 3 – that send messages to each other on directed channels, together with an *environment node*, Node 0, which will be responsible for initiating the algorithm.

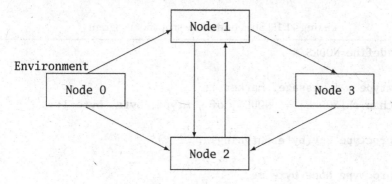

Fig. 11.3. A directed graph of nodes

A random simulation of the PROMELA program from the next section gave the following output for the snapshot:

```
Node 1, last sent to 2 = 2
Node 1, last received from 2 = 7
Messages in channel 2 -> 1 = 8 .. 12
Node 1, last sent to 3 = 17
        Node 3, last received from 1 = 17
        Node 3, last sent to 2 = 6
    Node 2, last sent to 1 = 12
    Node 2, last received from 1 = 2
    Node 2, last received from 3 = 3
    Messages in channel 3 -> 2 = 4 .. 6
```

Check the consistency of the snapshot. For example, Node 2 sent messages 0 through 12 to Node 1; of these messages, 0 through 7 were received by Node 1, while messages 8 through 12 remained in the channel.

11.7 The Chandy–Lamport snapshot algorithm in PROMELA

The implementation of the snapshot algorithm is somewhat complex, but it is worth studying in order to see how the constructs of PROMELA work together in a large program. It is also instructive to compare the straightforward implementation of the algorithm in this section with a model designed for efficient verification that is presented in Section 11.8. Since the program is long, it will be presented in segments. The implementation of PrintState can be found in the software archive.

An alternate implementation of the snapshot algorithm is given in the software archive for *PCDP*: four separate processes are used to model each

Listing 11.15. Structure of the snapshot program

```
1   #define NODES 4
2
3   mtype = { message, marker };
4   chan ch[NODES] = [NODES] of { mtype, byte, byte };
5
6   proctype Env(byte outgoing) { ... }
7
8   proctype Node(byte me;
9       byte numIncoming; byte incoming;
10      byte numOutgoing; byte outgoing) {
11  do
12  :: /* Send a message */
13  :: /* Receive a message */
14  :: /* Receive a marker */
15  :: markerCount == numIncoming ->
16          PrintState();
17          break
18  od
19  }
20
21  init {
22    atomic {
23      run Env(4+2);
24      run Node(1, 2, 4+1, 2, 8+4);
25      run Node(2, 3, 8+2+1, 1, 2);
26      run Node(3, 1, 2, 1, 4)
27    }
28  }
```

node instead of the one process per node used here, and the identities of incoming and outgoing channels are stored in channels instead of the bit encoding used here.

11.7.1 Structure of the program

The overall structure of the program is shown in Listing 11.15. The algorithm is implemented as a single process per node; there is one **proctype** for the environment node (line 6) and a separate one for the other nodes (lines 8–19).

A nondeterministic selection of alternatives implements the four processes described in the previous section (lines 12–17).

The source code for the environment node is given in Listing 11.16, while the expansion of the comments for three of the four alternatives (lines 12–14) is given in Listings 11.17 through 11.19. The fourth alternative (lines 15–17) is executed to terminate the process for the node when markers have been received on all the incoming channels. The processes themselves are activated in an **init** process (lines 21–28); the first parameter is the ID of the node and the other parameters are explained in the next subsection.

An array of channels is defined (lines 3–4), one for sending messages to each node. The messages are triples composed of: (1) a message type declared as an **mtype** with two values: message for a normal data message and marker for the marker used in the snapshot algorithm; (2) a byte for the index of the source node that is sending the message; and (3) a byte for the message sequence number.

11.7.2 Encoding lists of channels

How should the topology of the distributed system be represented? Each node needs to know the identities of its incoming and outgoing channels. For example, in the diagram in Figure 11.3, Node 2 has three incoming channels – to Node 0, Node 1, and Node 3 – but only one outgoing channel – to Node 1 – and this information is needed so that messages and markers will be sent and received only on these channels.

There are three ways that we can store a data structure that is a subset of the node IDs:

- An array of boolean flags: a flag is true if the node corresponding to the array index is in the subset.
- A channel that contains the subset of the node IDs.
- An integer variable that encodes the subset: a bit is 1 if the position of the bit is in the subset.

The array implementation is straightforward but inefficient because SPIN does not pack an array of bits, so an array of boolean flags is implemented as an array of bytes. Section 11.1 demonstrated the use of channels to store data structures; here we demonstrate the third method.

Let us assume that there are at most eight nodes so that we can store the indices of each subset of node IDs in a single byte, where bit i (starting from the low-order bit) is 1 if node i is in the subset. For example, for Node 2 in the diagram in Figure 11.3, the sets of incoming and outgoing channels are represented by

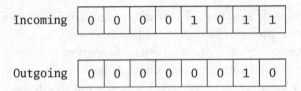

Incoming	0	0	0	0	1	0	1	1

Outgoing	0	0	0	0	0	0	1	0

These values are used to initialize the parameters incoming and outgoing in the processes for the nodes (lines 6, 9–10, 23–26 of Listing 11.15). Additional parameters numIncoming and numOutgoing give the *number* of incoming and outgoing channels; this is done for simplicity and is redundant because their values could be computed by counting the bits whose value is 1. What is important in this design is that the initialization of the model to a specific network topology is encapsulated within the **init** process, while the processes for the nodes are independent of the topology.

To check if a channel exists, we need to check if the corresponding bit is 1. This is done by shifting the byte by a number of places equal to the index of the channel and then masking the lowest-order bit. It is convenient to define a macro to do this calculation:

```
#define isOne(v,n) (v >> n & 1)
```

The macro is used in guards: line 5 in Listing 11.16 and line 14 in Listing 11.19.

> ## Warning
>
> **inline** cannot be called from an expression.

11.7.3 The environment node

The code for the environment node is very simple; it simply sends a marker on all outgoing channels (Listing 11.16). The global variable startSnapshot is used just to obtain interesting simulations of the program. It blocks the execution of the environment process (line 2) until a reasonable number of messages have been sent by the nonenvironment nodes.

11.7.4 Local data for each node

The data required by the algorithm are stored in variables declared as local variables in the **proctype** Node:

Listing 11.16. The environment node

```
1  proctype Env(byte outgoing) {
2    startSnapshot;
3    for (I, 1, NODES-1)
4      if
5      :: isOne(outgoing,I) ->
6             ch[I] ! marker, 0, 0;
7      :: else
8      fi
9    rof (I)
10 }
```

```
byte lastSent[NODES];
byte lastReceived[NODES];
byte stateAtRecord[NODES];
byte messageAtRecord[NODES];
byte messageAtMarker[NODES];
```

The declarations are arrays because they store message numbers sent on outgoing channels or received from incoming channels, and a node may be connected to every other node.

Two other variables are needed by the algorithm:

```
byte markerCount;
bool recorded;
```

markerCount counts the number of incoming markers; when markers have been received on all incoming edges, its value equals numIncoming and the process can print the state and terminate (lines 15–17 in Listing 11.15). recorded is a flag that is used to ensure that a state is recorded only once.

Several variables are not strictly part of the algorithm but are needed to write the program:

```
byte messageNumber;
byte destination;
byte source;
byte received;
```

The algorithm is modeled by sending messages consisting of a single integer value, and messageNumber is used to generate the sequence of message numbers. The other three variables are temporary variables used to store channel and message numbers needed in the send and receive statements.

Listing 11.17. Sending a message

```
1   :: numOutgoing != 0 ->
2      GetOutgoing();
3      if
4      :: full(ch[destination])
5      :: nfull(ch[destination]) ->
6         ch[destination] ! message(me, messageNumber);
7         lastSent[destination] = messageNumber;
8         messageNumber++;
9         if
10        :: messageNumber > MESSAGES ->
11           startSnapshot = true
12        :: else
13        fi
14     fi
```

11.7.5 Nodes of the distributed system

We now turn to the three alternatives in the Node processes. Listing 11.17 shows the alternative for sending a message (line 12 in Listing 11.15). Line 1 ensures that the code will still work even if a node is a sink with no outgoing channels. Line 2 chooses an arbitrary destination node; this is not at all easy to do and is discussed separately in Section 11.7.6. A message is sent on the channel destination (line 6), but only if that channel is not full (line 5). Note the use of the alternate syntax for send statements: the **mtype** field followed by the other fields in parentheses. Lines 9–13 unblock the environment process to start the snapshot after a certain number of messages (MESSAGES) has been sent. All processes can execute these statements, though only one is needed; repeatedly setting the variable startSnapshot to **true** does no harm.

The next two alternatives (Listings 11.18 and 11.19) check the first message in the node's incoming channel to see if it is a message or a marker. The receive statements (line 1 of both listings) have a *value* as the first argument, so only the statement that matches the first message in the channel will be executable. Since there is only one channel per node, the source node of the message is included as a field, so that the receiving node can attribute it to the correct incoming channel.

The code for receiving a message is easy and just requires that we store its sequence number (Listing 11.18).

Listing 11.18. Receiving a message

```
1  :: ch[me] ? message(source, received) ->
2        lastReceived[source] = received;
```

When a marker is received (Listing 11.19), the number of the last message received is stored as required by the algorithm (line 2). markerCount is incremented (line 3) and is used by the fourth alternative to determine if the process can be terminated. There are now two possibilities: (a) a marker has already been received and the state recorded so there is nothing more to do (line 5), or (b) this is the first marker encountered. In the second case, the state is recorded (lines 7–11) and then markers are sent on all outgoing channels (line 12–18). If the state has already been recorded, the value stored in messageAtMarker will likely be greater than that previously stored in messageAtRecord. The difference between the two is the number of messages that will be attributed to the channel in the snapshot.

Listing 11.19. Receiving a marker

```
1  :: ch[me] ? marker(source, _) ->
2        messageAtMarker[source] = lastReceived[source];
3        markerCount++;
4        if
5        :: recorded -> skip
6        :: else ->
7              recorded = true;
8              for (I, 0, NODES-1)
9                 stateAtRecord[I] = lastSent[I];
10                messageAtRecord[I] = lastReceived[I]
11             rof (I);
12             for (J, 0, NODES-1)
13                if
14                :: isOne(outgoing,J) ->
15                      ch[J] ! marker(me, 0)
16                :: else
17                fi
18             rof (J)
19       fi
```

Listing 11.20. Nondeterministic choice of a channel

```
1   inline GetOutgoing() {
2     atomic {
3       byte num, out;
4       num = numOutgoing;
5       out = outgoing;
6       destination = 0;
7       do
8       :: (out & 1) == 0 ->
9             out = out >> 1;
10            destination++
11      :: (out & 1) == 1) ->
12            break
13      :: ((out & 1) == 1) && (num > 1) ->
14            num--;
15            out = out >> 1;
16            destination++
17      od
18    }
19  }
```

11.7.6 Nondeterministic choice of a channel

If the topology of the network were coded within each node, a simple nondeterministic **if**-statement would suffice for choosing a destination for sending a message:

```
/* Choose destination in Node 1 */
if
:: destination = 2
:: destination = 3
fi
```

This is much more difficult to do if we want the code for each node to be identical, but the basic idea is the same, as shown in the **inline** sequence GetOutgoing (Listing 11.20). Each bit is examined in turn: if it is 0, skip to the next bit (lines 8–10), but if it is 1, nondeterministically select whether to use this channel (lines 11–12) or to look for the next one (lines 13–16). The result of the execution of the algorithm is a channel number in the variable destination that is used in Listing 11.17. The variable num (initialized from numOutgoing) ensures that skipping over a channel is not done if this is the last outgoing channel (line 13).

The code is executed only if numOutgoing is greater than zero (line 1 in Listing 11.17) so we don't have to worry that a channel will not be found. The code is placed within **atomic** because it is just computing on local variables that cannot be affected by other processes. The values of outgoing and numOutgoing are copied into the variables out and num, respectively, so that the new variables can be used for computation without affecting the values stored in the original ones.

> ### Warning
>
> *Do not* try to initialize these variables in their declarations (line 3); if you do so, they will be initialized once at the beginning of the process and not again, because **inline** does not introduce a new scope.

11.8 Verification of the snapshot algorithm

The program for the snapshot algorithm given in the previous section is too complex to verify efficiently. Rather than verifying the *program*, we need to construct a *model* for the algorithm and verify the model instead.

A bit of thought should convince you that the correctness of the *algorithm* is independent of the number of nodes and channels. It is true that we may make *programming* errors in the loops and indices needed to keep track of the sets of incoming and outgoing channels, but as far as the algorithm is concerned, it is sufficient to check its behavior on a single channel. In principle, a second channel is needed in order to model the case where a marker has been received on one channel (and the state recorded) before the marker is received on another channel. But it is not necessary to model the reception of the first marker using a channel! It is sufficient if the action of recording the state can occur at an arbitrary control point in the algorithm, and this is easily modeled by nondeterministic selection.

The model will use two processes, a Sender and a Receiver connected by a single channel. They use the following global variables:

```
mtype = { message, marker };
chan ch = [SIZE] of { mtype, byte };

byte lastSent, lastReceived,
     messageAtRecord, messageAtMarker;
bool recorded;
```

The messages in the channel contain only the message type and number because there is only one sending process. The other variables are familiar from the algorithm. They are declared globally so that they can be referred to in correctness specifications.

The Sender process (Listing 11.21) sends a fixed number of messages (lines 3–5); nondeterministically, it can also choose to send a marker (line 6). Once the marker is sent, we know that the receiver will record its state, so the sender process can terminate.

Listing 11.21. Verifying the snapshot algorithm (the sending process)

```
1  active proctype Sender() {
2    do
3    :: lastSent < MESSAGES ->
4         lastSent++;
5         ch ! message(lastSent)
6    :: ch ! marker(0) ->
7         break
8    od
9  }
```

The receiver (Listing 11.22) receives either a message (lines 4–5) or a marker (lines 6–13) and updates its variables as specified by the algorithm. There is a third alternative in the **do**-statement (lines 14–16): at any time before the state has been recorded, the receiver node can record its state. The flag recorded is used (line 9) to prevent recording the state a second time when the marker is received.

To complete the model we have to specify the channel capacity SIZE and the number of messages sent MESSAGES. Even if the system we plan to build has a large channel capacity, its full capacity need not be modeled. It is well known that bugs tend to occur at the limits of a data structure, for example, when it is empty or when it is full. If we choose SIZE to be four, we can claim

Listing 11.22. Verifying the snapshot algorithm (the receiving process)

```
1   active proctype Receiver() {
2     byte received;
3     do
4     :: ch ? message(received) ->
5          lastReceived = received
6     :: ch ? marker(_) ->
7          messageAtMarker = lastReceived;
8          if
9          :: !recorded ->
10             messageAtRecord = lastReceived
11         :: else
12         fi;
13         break
14    :: !recorded ->
15         messageAtRecord = lastReceived;
16         recorded = true
17    od
18  }
```

to have verified the algorithm if the marker is sent before or after the first or the last element, as well as "in the middle":

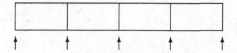

Choosing a larger value would not increase our confidence in the algorithm: if it works when the marker is in the "middle" of the channel, it should also work if the "middle" is larger.

We also have to choose the number of MESSAGES to the sent. Sending six messages seems to be reasonable. Clearly you wouldn't send fewer messages than the channel capacity, because then you would not check the case of a full channel; furthermore, there is no need to send more than one or two messages beyond those needed to fill the channel.

What properties do we need to prove to verify the model of the snapshot algorithm? Termination of the algorithm follows easily from the fact that the graph is connected, so let us concentrate on verifying the safety of the algorithm, namely, that the snapshot is consistent.

The algorithm only works if the channels are FIFO. It follows from the semantics of PROMELA that the messages are received in FIFO order, but you can add:

```
assert (received == (lastReceived+1))
```

after line 4 in Listing 11.22 to be sure.

The consistency of the snapshot follows from two assertions placed after the **do**-statement in the receiver (line 17 of Listing 11.22):

```
assert (lastSent == messageAtMarker);
assert (messageAtRecord <= messageAtMarker)
```

The first assertion states that all messages sent before the marker have been received. It is of course possible that the state had already been recorded when the marker was received on the channel; in that case, the messages between messageAtRecord and messageAtMarker are attributed to the channel rather than to one of the nodes. Since we are assured that messages are received in FIFO order, it is sufficient to check the expression in second assertion.

A SPIN verification of this model is immediate, as only about 3000 states have to be checked.

A

Software Tools

The first section of this Appendix describes how to install SPIN. The following sections present an overview of the SPIN-based tools that I have developed. The tools are written in JAVA and distributed both as source code and as compiled jar files that can be run directly. For more detail on each tool, consult the documentation that is included in the distributions. All this software can be freely downloaded from the websites whose addresses are listed in Appendix B.

A.1 SPIN

SPIN can be downloaded as an executable file for WINDOWS and LINUX. You can also download the source code and build it for any system that has an ANSI C compiler.

A C compiler is needed to compile the verifier programs that SPIN generates. In WINDOWS, gcc can be installed as part of CYGWIN, a LINUX-like environment. If you do not wish to install the CYGWIN environment, gcc can be obtained as part of the MINGW (Minimalist GNU for Windows) toolset. Download and open the following archives in the order given:

```
binutils-N.tar.gz
gcc-core-N.tar.gz
mingw-runtime-N.tar.gz
w32api-N.tar.gz
```

where N is the version and build number. It is acceptable if some files are overwritten when the archives are opened.

The environment variable Path should be set to include the directories containing the SPIN executable file and the C compiler (for MINGW, this

Fig. A.1. The JSPIN integrated development environment

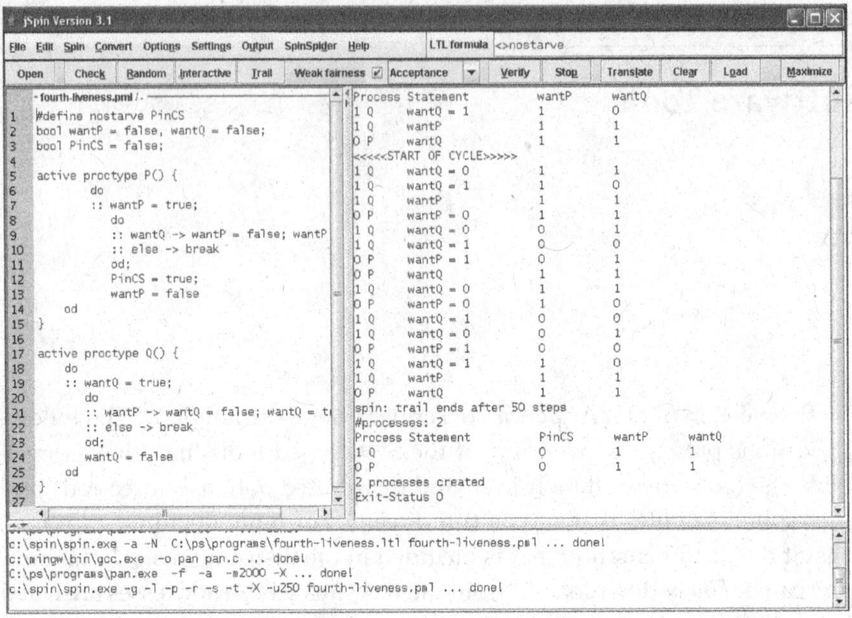

defaults to c:\mingw\bin). The variable can be changed from the window obtained by selecting:

```
Start/Control Panel/System/Advanced/Environment Variables/PATH
```

You are now ready to use SPIN as a command-line tool.

A.2 JSPIN

JSPIN is an integrated development environment for SPIN with a graphical user interface (Figure A.1). The user interface consists of a single window with menus, a toolbar and three adjustable panes where text is displayed. All menu and toolbar commands have keyboard mnemonics or accelerators. The left pane is used to display PROMELA source files. The lower pane is used to display messages from both SPIN and JSPIN. The right pane is used to display the output from **printf** statements, messages from SPIN (in particular those concerning verification), and displays of data from random, interactive, and guided simulations.

Most of the arguments used by SPIN are supplied automatically by JSPIN, so that you only have to select a button to execute SPIN in one of its modes.

You can explicitly add to or modify the arguments by selecting from the Options menu.

During simulation runs the SPIN output is filtered and appears in the right pane in tabular form, one state per line, as described in Sections 3.1.1 and 2.2.2.

JSPIN contains commands for translating formulas in linear temporal logic into never claims and incorporating them into verification runs (Section 5.3.3).

JSPIN is implemented using the SWING library of JAVA for building graphical user interfaces. SPIN, the C compiler, and the verifiers are run by forking subprocesses to execute commands that are built with the proper arguments. The textual output from the subprocesses is piped back to JSPIN for filtering and display.

The SPINSPIDER tool described in the next section is integrated into JSPIN, although it can also be run independently from the command line.

A.3 SPINSPIDER

SPINSPIDER is a software tool for automatically generating the state transition diagram of a PROMELA program (Figure 4.1). When SPIN performs a verification, it searches the full state space and sufficient information is available on the search to enable the construction of the state diagram. SPINSPIDER works with four input files (Figure A.2):

- the PROMELA source file;
- the debug file obtained by running a verification of the program with the -DCHECK option and with a never claim that prints out the program counters and variable values;
- the statement file obtained by running a verification with the -d option;
- the trail file of a computation.

The debug file traces the search state by state. It contains data written by a special never claim in the source file; this claim is constructed automatically from information (the number of processes and the variable names) supplied interactively when running SPINSPIDER. The source file and the statement file are used to translate codes in the debug file so that the location counters can be displayed with a line number and the source code. These data are used to create a description of the state diagram in dot graphics format. Then, the DOT program is called to layout the diagram and to convert it to a displayable graphics format such as PNG. Optionally, the trail file of a computation can be used to emphasize a path within in the state diagram or to display a diagram consisting only of a single path.

Fig. A.2. The structure of SPINSPIDER

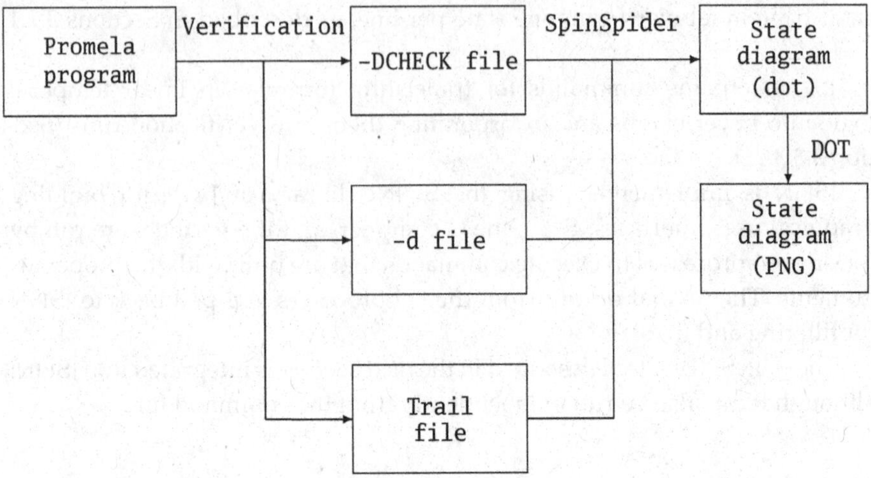

Figure A.3 shows the state diagram that was automatically generated for the program in Listing 5.2 described in Section 5.5. Recall that that program terminates but only for weakly fair computations. Attempting to verify the LTL formula <>flag results in an error and the trail is used to emphasize the cycle in the diagram corresponding to an infinite path.

A.4 VN: Visualizing nondeterminism

The use of the VN software tool for visualizing nondeterminism was described in Section 8.2.

The structure of VN is shown in Figure A.4. An NDFA is first constructed interactively using the JFLAP tool and saved in the XML format that JFLAP defines. VN reads this file and displays the NDFA. A PROMELA program similar to that in Listing 8.1 is generated from the NDFA and an input string. Depending on the mode selected: Random, Create, Find or Next, the appropriate commands are built and subprocesses forked. Output from the subprocesses is piped to VN and used to display computations.

VN writes instructions for drawing the NDFA and the paths in the dot graphical format, and then calls the DOT tool to lay out the graphs and to convert them into PNG format for display.

Fig. A.3. State diagram generated by SPINSPIDER

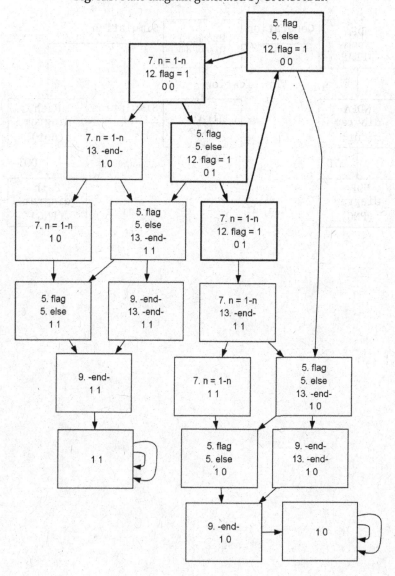

Fig. A.4. The structure of VN

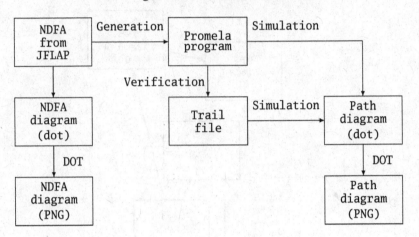

B

Links

Websites for software

CYGWIN	cygwin.com
DTSPIN	www.win.tue.nl/~dragan/DTSpin
GRAPHVIZ (DOT)	graphviz.org
JFLAP	jflap.org
JSPIN, SPINSPIDER	sourceforge.net/projects/pcdp,
	stwww.weizmann.ac.il/g-cs/benari/jspin
MINGW	mingw.org
SPARK	www.sparkada.com
SPIN	spinroot.com
Temporal logic patterns	patterns.projects.cis.ksu.edu
UPPAAL	uppaal.com
VN	sourceforge.net/projects/pcdp,
	stwww.weizmann.ac.il/g-cs/benari/vn

Websites for books

Principles of the Spin Model Checker	www.springer.com/978-1-84628-769-5
Mathematical Logic for Computer Science	stwww.weizmann.ac.il/g-cs/benari/books
Principles of Concurrent and Distributed Programming	www.pearsoned.co.uk/ben-ari
The Spin Model Checker	spinroot.com/spin/Doc/Book_extras

References

1. Krzysztof R. Apt and Ernst-Rüdiger Olderog. *Verification of Sequential and Concurrent Programs*. Springer, Berlin, 1991.
2. Michal Armoni and Judith Gal-Ezer. Introducing non-determinism. *Journal of Computers in Mathematics and Science Teaching*, 25(4):325–359, 2006.
3. John Barnes. *High Integrity Software: The SPARK Approach to Safety and Security*. Addison-Wesley, Harlow, UK, 2003.
4. M. Ben-Ari. *Principles of Concurrent and Distributed Programming (Second Edition)*. Addison-Wesley, Harlow, UK, 2006.
5. Mordechai Ben-Ari. *Mathematical Logic for Computer Science (Second Edition)*. Springer, London, 2001.
6. Mordechi Ben-Ari and Alan Burns. Extreme interleavings. *IEEE Concurrency*, 6(3):90, 1998.
7. K.M. Chandy and L. Lamport. Distributed snapshots: Determining global states of distributed systems. *ACM Transactions on Computer Systems*, 3(1):63–75, 1985.
8. Edmund M. Clarke, Orna Grumberg, and Doron A. Peled. *Model Checking*. MIT Press, Cambridge, MA, 1999.
9. Matthew B. Dwyer, George S. Avrunin, and James C. Corbett. Patterns in property specifications for finite-state verification. In *21st International Conference on Software Engineering*, pages 411–420, 1999.
10. Robert W. Floyd. Nondeterministic algorithms. *Journal of the ACM*, 14(4):636–644, 1967.
11. C.A.R. Hoare. *Communicating Sequential Processes*. Prentice Hall International, Hemel Hempstead, UK, 1985/2004. http://www.usingcsp.com/cspbook.pdf.
12. Gerard J. Holzmann. *The Spin Model Checker: Primer and Reference Manual*. Addison-Wesley, Reading, MA, 2004.
13. Mike Jones. What really happened on Mars Rover Pathfinder. *The Risks Digest*, 19(49), 1997. http://catless.ncl.ac.uk/Risks/19.49.html.
14. Jane W. S. Liu. *Real-Time Systems*. Prentice Hall, Upper Saddle River, NJ, 2000.
15. Nancy A. Lynch. *Distributed Algorithms*. Morgan Kaufman, San Francisco, CA, 1996.

16. Z. Manna and A. Pnueli. *The Temporal Logic of Reactive and Concurrent Systems: Specification*. Springer, New York, 1992.

17. Z. Manna and A. Pnueli. *Temporal Verification of Reactive Systems: Safety*. Springer, New York, 1995.

18. Susan H. Rodger and Thomas W. Finley. *JFLAP: An Interactive Formal Languages and Automata Package*. Jones & Bartlett, Sudbury, MA, 2006.

19. Theo C. Ruys. *Towards Effective Model Checking*. PhD thesis, University of Twente, 2001. http://wwwhome.cs.utwente.nl/~ruys/ruys-phd-thesis.pdf.

Index